*Dear Rose &
my fami[ly]
very much! R[...]
celebrate life & you'll have a life worth
celebrating!!
both
ays
Love,
Erin Ley
12/07*

The Will to Live

The Perks of Cancer Through the Eyes of a Survivor

Erin Ley

PublishAmerica
Baltimore

First printing

ISBN: 1-4241-8229-8
PUBLISHED BY PUBLISHAMERICA, LLLP
www.publishamerica.com
Baltimore

Printed in the United States of America

Endorsements

"After reading Erin Ley's *The Will to Live*, I would recommend it to any of my patients who are facing serious health problems. Erin takes us through her cancer with such clarity and spirit that *The Will to Live* will be an inspiration to anyone facing a dire illness or any potentially devastating situation. This book can give patients the hope and inspiration that we physicians cannot always provide."

– Romeo C. Solon, M.D., Lenox Hill Hospital, New York, NY

"*The Will to Live* is full of valuable information about how to cope with a cancer diagnosis and the treatments that follow, but Erin Ley's courageous, deeply personal account of her own experience as a cancer survivor is what makes this book unique. She tells the story of this chaotic period in her life—a roller coaster ride of physical and emotional highs and lows—calmly and with unflinching honesty. Erin's descriptions of her experiences are heartrending, but her unwavering determination to focus on her inner strength and optimism shine through every page. In *The Will to Live*, Erin Ley speaks from her heart, and I feel that her story will move and inspire cancer patients, their families, and their friends."

– Whoopi Goldberg, winner of an Academy Award, Golden Globe Award, Grammy Award, People's Choice Award, Tony Award, and many others; host of radio talk show *Wake Up With Whoopi;* tireless activist on behalf of children's issues, the homeless, human rights, substance abuse, the struggle against AIDS, and many others.

"Erin Ley's *The Will to Live* is a powerful and inspiring read for cancer patients and for those close to them. Individuals experience their own 'cancers'—tragedies that become defining moments—in their lives, and hopefully go on to become survivors. Erin focuses on living and thriving, not death and hopelessness. What an enthralling, refreshing read!"

– Itzhak Haimovic, M.D., F.A.A.N.

"*The Will to Live: The Perks of Cancer through the Eyes of a Survivor* is a well-documented and powerfully introspective insight into the mindset of a young adult living with, through and beyond cancer. Erin is clearly someone who got busy living when faced with her diagnosis and who serves as yet another one of myriad growing examples of what it means to survive cancer as a member of this oft-forgotten demographic."

– Matthew Zachary, Founder and Executive Director of Steps For Living, Inc., and Cancer Survivor

"Erin Ley has taken her early experience with life-threatening disease and turned it into a positive story of empowerment. Her journey from illness to a fulfilling career and family is a rewarding narrative."

– Paul Margulies, M.D., F.A.C.P., F.A.C.E., Clinical Associate Professor of Medicine, NYU School of Medicine; Attending Physician, Department of Medicine, North Shore University Hospital, Manhasset, NY

"Erin Ley's *The Will to Live* clearly describes how one's *positive* approach to disease and life can guide and help heal both physical illness and emotional conflict. It is an inspiring portrayal of how an individual's will, attitude, spirit and personal strength oftentimes are the difference between success and failure in the treatment of many illnesses. Bravo Erin!"

– Kenneth F. Mattucci, M.D., F.A.C.S.

"As a young adult with cancer Erin's world erupted in unexpected ways that tested her ability to transform loss into gain, deepen her will, and transform her life. Our ability to coexist with cancer and its lasting effects are very much influenced by what we do with the disease more than what the disease does to us. As Erin reflects on the lessons she took from cancer, she shares what healing really means with her readers."

– Selma Schimmel, CEO, Vital Options International and host of *The Group Room*® cancer talk radio show

"Erin Ley has transformed a life-threatening struggle and created an inspiring, moving and heartfelt journey of growth and wellness. With eloquence and grace of spirit, she has offered a priceless gift of healing."

– Debra Koppelman, Director of Development, Coalition Against Breast Cancer, Inc.

"With remarkable courage and humor, Erin Ley gives us a roadmap to healing mind and body; from the dreaded cancer diagnosis, through the harrowing medical maze, to the peace of recovery. *The Will to Live* is a 'must-read' for anyone facing such a challenge."

– Kathleen Atkinson, LSW-R, Psychotherapist, and Cancer Survivor

"... stirring. *The Will to Live* is a motivational journey that will inspire readers to readdress their own life's perspectives."

– Robert Herman, M.D., P.C

"*The Will To Live* shares the personality factors which can make one a survivor. There are qualities within survivors which help them to exceed expectations and become our teachers and guides when we confront adversity. This book is filled with the hard-earned wisdom of a survivor. Erin Ley writes about cancer introducing itself to her and improving her life. I think it introduced Erin to herself and she liked whom she met and fought for her life. She became what I call a *respant*, a responsible participant and not a patient, submissive sufferer. She shares the important lessons that one should never give up hope and always pay attention to the mind, heart and spirit, and to the possibilities which exist. I have learned that when mind, body and spirit work together in your life, they truly help you to heal your life and cure your disease."

– Bernie Siegel, M.D., author of *Love, Medicine & Miracles* and *Help Me To Heal*

With all my love, this book is dedicated to my aunt, Rita (McArdle) McNulty. In life and when faced with death, she demonstrated relentless courage and grace. Aunt Rita inspired me from the moment I was born, and continues to do so now as she rests in peace. Aunt Rita, a true lady, was one of a kind— unforgettable and irreplaceable. She will always hold a special place in my heart.

Contents

Acknowledgments

I would like to offer my sincerest heartfelt thanks to all of my family and friends, from the East Coast to the West Coast. Their love and devotion helped me get through the most tumultuous time in my life. My friends in Smithtown, New York, where I'm raising my family, have contributed to the quality of my life post-cancer. Everyone has shown great dedication while walking with me through my diagnosis, treatment, cure, and beyond.

I am incredibly thankful for my babysitters, who are part of the Gorham Lane family. I would not have been able to focus on completing this book without the help of Nicole, Victoria, and Gabrielle Cuccurullo.

I would also like to express my immense gratitude to my remarkable therapist, Marianne Muldoon, and to the many medical specialists who treated me from head to toe, with special thanks to my internist, Dr. Barbara DelliBovi (now retired). Their expertise and wealth of medical knowledge made me feel that I was in the very best of hands, and I know they'll be there to help me through any medical situations that I may encounter in the future.

Special thanks also to my brilliant oncologist, Dr. David Straus. It is because of him that I am alive today, and that my husband and I have been able to bring three other lives into the world. There are no words that could sufficiently convey my gratitude. The best I can do is to say thank you—with all my heart and soul.

Thank you also to everyone who has provided me with wonderful endorsements, and feedback about this book. Your support, encouragement, and suggestions have been invaluable, and have kept me going through the long writing process.

My greatest appreciation goes to my husband Ronnie and our miracle children, Brendan, Danny, and Maggie. I've read that miracles come in threes, and that is certainly apropos to my life. My husband and our children have brought my new and improved life to even greater heights. They inspire me every day—each in their own way—and have shown great patience while I have been writing this book. I love you all, always and forever.

Foreword

I first met Erin (Heenan) Ley when we were beginning our junior year of high school in Garden City, New York. Erin always loves a good time and always has a smile on her face—she's a very approachable person. We also had a lot in common, so Erin and I quickly became best friends; we have remained so to this day.

We were only twenty-five years old when Erin was diagnosed with a life-threatening form of cancer—non-Hodgkins lymphoma—in May 1991. I was shocked—how this could happen to anyone our age, and to Erin of all people, was beyond my comprehension. As I watched Erin go through the demanding treatments that tested her courage, faith, and physical, emotional, and mental strength to their limits, all I kept thinking was that she *had* to get better. I knew Erin was an incredibly strong person, so I believed with all my heart that her physical and mental strength would make her healthy again.

This book is Erin's story of her personal journey through cancer. She writes candidly about the many ups and downs she experienced—hope and despair, joy and distress, bravery and fear, tranquility and anger. Nevertheless, when Erin looks back and discusses those times with me, she always says she is grateful to have had the experience, and that it changed the direction of her life for the better.

The time Erin spent living with cancer gave her a priceless gift—the willingness and ability to look for the silver lining, no matter how difficult things get. Her diagnosis and treatments took her on a journey that tested this ability to the limit. Her life-and-death battle with non-Hodgkins lymphoma was the catalyst that prompted her to explore the deepest parts of herself, where she found strength and wisdom she didn't know she had. With great admiration, I watched the strongest person I know keep getting stronger and stronger during the most difficult time of her life. And more than ten years later, when I was diagnosed with breast cancer, I drew strength from my memories of Erin's struggle and ultimate success—they were so inspirational for me! Without realizing it, Erin had shared her priceless gift of optimism and faith with me.

When I told Erin about my diagnosis, she hopped right into the picture and played an amazing role in my journey with cancer. She made me realize that I *was* going to get through it, and that the cancer was not a death sentence. As Erin had shown me a little more than ten years before, it's mind over matter. With her help and encouragement, and with the incredible support of my husband Jerry, my will to live became bigger and greater than anything else. Cancer was the enemy, and I was going to beat this enemy. After radiation, a double mastectomy, numerous operations, seemingly endless medication, and everyone tilting their head asking me if I was okay, I finally got through it—I became a survivor. I ask myself to this day, *What would I have done without her?*

Now that all of the craziness is over, I want to thank Erin for her uplifting conversations and the gift of a St. Peregrine medal (the patron saint of cancer patients), which I keep in my wallet at all times. Erin showed me that when you recognize how strong you really are, you can battle anything. She helped me to see that I needed to grow stronger, grow as a woman, and realize that nothing would take me away from my life. And that is exactly what I did—with Erin's support, I drew upon my never-ending physical, mental, and spiritual strength.

In this book, Erin does not minimize the physical and emotional pain and fear experienced by patients, their families, and their friends. On the contrary, she writes with searing honesty about the debilitating effects that her diagnosis and treatment regime had on her and everyone around her. As we, her loved ones, were helping her through this trying time in her life, she was doing the same for us. We were drawing strength from each other.

I realized Erin's strength as a woman when she lost her "crowning glory" hair, eyebrows, and eyelashes. I went with her to help her pick out wigs. That must have been a devastating experience for her, but she continued to smile and glow as the beautiful woman that she truly is. We actually had fun with it—Erin and I had so many laughs that day. Who would think?

The most inspiring part of Erin's message is that in the midst of all the pain, fear, and sometimes despair, she was able to find many positive things—important practical lessons, insights into herself and her relationships with loved ones, and the power and beauty of hope for the future. These are what Erin calls the perks of cancer. This book does not recount her experiences in chronological order. Instead, each section explains how Erin recognized and gradually embraced one of these perks, and how each has contributed to her development as a person.

This book is a gold mine of information, support, and inspiration for cancer patients, their families, and everyone who would like to more fully understand what a diagnosis of cancer means at the most intimate, personal level. In it, Erin gives practical advice on everything from coping with hair loss to how to tell strangers that you have cancer, and heartfelt words of support to others who find their lives turned upside down by a diagnosis of serious illness.

Ultimately, this book is about what Erin learned about herself, about others, and about the world while battling a life-threatening illness. It tells the story of one person's experience, but its message is universal—out of pain and despair, we can always find joy and hope if we are willing to look for them.

Thank you, Erin, for making my life richer and better than it has ever been before.

Kristin Linn Voels, Cancer Survivor

Introduction
How Cancer Introduced Itself to Me

I opened my eyes, sat straight up in my bed, and looked out the window, curious about what kind of day lay before me. After a few moments, the weather registered. It was another beautiful day in April, and I was ready to meet it head on. I began my regular routine of showering, dressing, and leaving for work with a bagel in my mouth. As I drove, relaxed, I listened to the radio, thought about the exciting weekend I had lined up, and began coughing.

When I arrived at the office where I worked with a broker/dealer as an account executive for an insurance company, I reviewed my list of potential clients while drinking a cup of tea. Then, I headed to my administrator's office and bumped into my supervisor in the hallway.

"Good morning, Erin," he said.

"Hi there." I rested my hand on the wall. I felt faint for a moment and then it passed.

"Are you okay?" he asked, concern pinching the skin between his brows. A very kind and gracious gentleman, he genuinely seemed to care about the well-being of his employees.

Smiling, I responded, "Sure. I just have some funny chest pains, but I'm all right."

"It's probably from stress," he said. "You've been working hard over the last week or so. Maybe you should take it easy."

"Take it easy? What does that mean again?" I joked. "It's a busy week and I have a list of potential clients, meetings and lunches. Don't worry; it's all good." I assured him before continuing down the hallway.

Once I was back in my office, I began feeling pains in my shoulder and down my arm. I thought about my father, who'd survived a heart attack at forty-nine years old, and even though I was only twenty-five, I did not want to take any chances. I immediately gathered my belongings, left the office, and headed for the hospital.

When I arrived at the emergency room, the doctor gave me a haphazard examination and diagnosed me with stress. He wrote me a prescription for codeine pills to be taken for one week. *Since when do codeine pills help with stress?* I wondered. *Am I even stressed?* I hadn't thought so. But because the person who prescribed them wore the requisite white coat symbolizing expertise, I felt it was my duty to trust in his care.

For me, the codeine pills proved to be nothing more than a depressant. They left me feeling groggy and overly sensitive. Nonetheless, because they were supposed to cure me of my chest pains and cough, I continued to comply. As time went on, however, my cough deepened, the chest pains occurred more frequently, I became increasingly lightheaded, and I felt fatigued much more than usual.

I had no idea what was happening to me, so I went back to the hospital, where I was seen by the same doctor.

I hoped he would remember me so I wouldn't have to go through the whole "stress and codeine" story.

He said that he did and asked me why I was back.

"My symptoms are getting worse," I explained. "My cough, the lightheadedness, thhh—"

The doctor cut me off and told me my symptoms were stress-related. His tone was firm and unwavering. He seemed annoyed, as if I was wasting his time.

"I think it would be a good idea to have a chest x-ray," I said.

He disagreed.

"Why not?"

He said he had examined me and found nothing wrong.

"Well, I'm not getting up until the chest x-ray is ordered," I insisted. Suddenly, I was certain that I should not be leaving my fate in his hands. As uncharacteristic as it was of me to assert myself with an authority figure, I did. My feeling ill, combined with his utter lack of concern, was upsetting enough to rouse me from my usual behavior. "I'm twenty-five years old," I continued. "The only stress in my life right now is arranging my social calendar."

He bet his doctor's license there was nothing wrong with me and insisted an x-ray would be a waste of his time and mine.

"How can you say that?" I exclaimed, flabbergasted by his remark and his lack of professionalism. I thought he should take the x-ray for the sake of prudence, if nothing else! I became determined not to leave the hospital without having the test done. "Please order the x-ray," I insisted.

Despite his agitation, the doctor finally ordered the x-ray. He then went about his business. After having the x-ray, I went back to the hospital bed in the emergency room where my belongings were. I awaited the results.

About half an hour later the doctor came back to where I was. He informed me that I had a small shadow next to my heart. The report said it was mitral valve prolapse, which is very common in women and seemingly unrelated to my symptoms. Before I could comment, he said my symptoms were being caused by stress. Nevertheless, he wanted me to go see a doctor to follow up on the mitral valve prolapse. He handed me a piece of paper with a doctor's name and number on it.

"Wow," I responded. "Okay, thanks. At least now I know it's nothing to worry about."

Within a week, I went to the doctor to whom he referred me. He confirmed that I had mitral valve prolapse (MVP).

About three weeks later, I ended up in a pulmonologist's office. I'd been finding it increasingly difficult to breathe when lying down, and suddenly one night I couldn't do it at all. I explained to the doctor what had been happening and informed him of the "stress" diagnosis. He sent me for a CT scan. After the scan, my breathing became even more difficult. I went into anaphylactic shock, caused by an allergic reaction to the CT scan dye, and found myself back in the emergency room.

The pulmonologist met me at the hospital and informed me that I had a large mass in my chest around the mediastinum, which seemed to be crushing my windpipe whenever I lay down. He said I'd need to stay in the hospital for extensive testing.

It immediately became clear to me that I had been misdiagnosed from the beginning. My symptoms had not been a result of stress, and the small shadow next to my heart was not MVP—it was the early stages of a tumor that had grown into a large mass during the month since my first emergency room visit.

After making that deduction, I looked across the crowded emergency room where I sat, once again, and saw the same doctor whose mistake and "hurry up and get out" attitude had allowed the deterioration of my health. When our eyes met, the fury I felt was indescribable. With all the strength I had left, I looked him in the eye and screamed, "Stay the hell away from me! You never took my complaints seriously, not even for a minute! Stress? Codeine? Did you cheat your way through medical school?"

I looked around at the other doctors and nurses. "Keep that guy away from me!" I shouted. "Don't let him near me! Do you hear me? *Don't let him near me!*"

In addition to feeling perfectly justified, my outburst was probably a way to release some of the overwhelming fear and anxiety that had come with this new diagnosis. Needless to say, the doctor stayed far away from me.

Once I calmed down, the pulmonologist began extensive testing to try to determine what exactly the mass was. I received blood test after blood test and numerous chest-needle biopsies, in which a large needle is inserted into the breastbone and you're slipped under a CT scan, where you undergo a series of tests. When the CT scan is finished, the doctor scoops out pieces of bone from the sternum and then removes the needle. This procedure, which is incredibly painful to have done just once, was repeated several times in a row in different parts of my sternum.

When all that was done, the diagnosis was in. Cancer.

When I first heard the word "cancer" spoken by my pulmonologist, I immediately assumed I was receiving a death sentence. My life flashed before my eyes, and everything I'd ever wanted to accomplish seemed suddenly out of reach. I could not accept the notion of losing those I loved. I went into a panic, unable to gather my thoughts. The only thing my body was capable of doing at that point was gathering what was left of its diminishing strength to utter what seemed like a bottomless, gut-wrenching *"Nooooooo!"*

By this time, my parents had already learned of the diagnosis. The pulmonologist asked them to wait down the hall until he informed me himself. My parents were told it could make things worse if they were in the room with me. But, to this day, they seem haunted when they recall hearing my heart-wrenching scream. Nevertheless, they were a great source of comfort when they were finally permitted to enter my room, only to find me curled up in a ball, filled with fear and confusion. I don't remember what was said at that point, but I do remember the relief I felt that they were with me.

Later that night, a priest came to my room. Unfamiliar with the hospital routines, I misinterpreted the purpose of his informal visit. As a Roman Catholic, I was certain he was there to anoint me with the final sacrament—the Last Rites. My heart stopped when he approached my bed, my breathing became rapid, and through my tears I ordered him out of the room and told him never to come back. Afterwards, I shook for hours. I was not ready to meet my Maker, nor was I prepared to say goodbye to my life.

I was, however, about to say goodbye to my life as I knew it. Prepared or not, the moment I received my diagnosis my life was altered forever.

When that day had begun, I was twenty-five years young, living at home with my family, and pretty much just drifting through life. My existence was not very deep. I was not the type who took the time to stop and smell the roses or to feel the velvety beauty of their soft petals. But, by nightfall, having received this horrific diagnosis, my sense of a future full of relatively carefree days had come to a jolting halt. As I tried to fall asleep, terror gave way to an imagined future of doctors and tests and treatments that would make me feel worse than I already did.

I had no way of knowing then that cancer would hardly be the end of my carefree life. In fact, more accurately, it heralded a new beginning—a less carefree approach and a more life-filled manner of living.

Perk 1
Making a New Beginning

At twenty-five years old I was thrown abruptly into a world of disease, pain, and emotional turmoil. My cancer came on suddenly and without warning, shattering the routine of my daily existence. It left me devastated to the core. Having spent my first twenty-five years without giving much thought to how I was living my life, I suddenly found myself face to face with my personal frailties and vulnerabilities. I was forced to reconsider the way I made decisions and existed in the world, realizing that every decision I made gave definition to who I was. My sense of time became less oriented toward some as yet undiscovered moment in the future. Instead, I felt the immediacy of past, present, and future all at once. As I began to take inventory of time wasted, I became acutely aware of the significance of every moment.

The insights I gained during this time and the months that followed transformed me so profoundly—and positively—that looking back

I see my diagnosis as the turning point in what essentially became "the beginning of the rest of my life."

Change didn't come about all at once, but I began to revise my priorities almost immediately, which led to many pivotal moments along the way that offered opportunities.

In May 1991, after the CT scan revealed the mass in my chest, I was admitted to the hospital. Although the doctors knew it was cancer, they were uncertain as to what kind. More tests had to be done. My family and I were distraught and unable to think clearly. My mother still relates how she ran around and around our kitchen table, devastated by the news. One of my best friends, Barbara, strongly recommended that my family and I switch hospitals as soon as possible. She had already lived through this as a teenager when her mother, Joan, was diagnosed with lymphoma, and knew that Memorial Sloan-Kettering Cancer Center (a.k.a. Sloan-Kettering) was a much better place to handle cancer than the hospital I was in. I thank God every day for her strength and direction at a time when my family needed it most.

Sloan-Kettering came highly recommended. After speaking with many people and hearing that cancer patients came to Sloan-Kettering from all over the world, it made sense to me and my family that it was the appropriate hospital for me. I had to wait a few weeks for the first available appointment with my new oncologist. The transition was not that bad. The physicians sent my records to Sloan-Kettering from the hospital I was in, and I made sure to provide whatever else was needed. The hard part was more the emotional and psychological adjusting and adapting that took place along the way.

For example, the pulmonologist, who was my only doctor at the time, initially said my treatment would probably consist of one month of radiation. I was distraught, yet at the same time relieved that I would not have to endure chemotherapy. But a few weeks later, after I'd made the change to Sloan-Kettering, more conclusive information began to mount up. It indicated that I had lymphoma, and it began to seem more likely that I'd be treated with six months of chemotherapy and radiation. As I was trying to adjust to this more distressing treatment plan, I was sent for a mediastinoscopy, a surgery in which my ribs were stretched apart, and the surgeon took a piece of the mass surrounding my breastbone. The doctors knew I had lymphoma, but had to determine which kind. After the surgery was done and all of the results were in, my diagnosis turned out to be non-Hodgkins lymphoblastic lymphoma, a rare pediatric cancer that is the cousin to (lymphoblastic) leukemia.

Following the surgery, a team of doctors entered my room and informed me that my protocol would be two and a half years of combination chemotherapy and one month of radiation. Every time I began to accept what I thought was as grueling a protocol as I could handle, I seemed to be given an even worse one. I finally cracked under the stress and did what my mother had done when she found out I had cancer. I walked around the room in circles, screaming and crying. I was unable to grasp the concept of a young woman—me—with cancer needing two and a half years of chemo and radiation. The doctors and nurses cried with me. As they apologized for being the bearers of bad news, an x-ray technician entered the room intending to perform a chest x-ray on me. I tried to comply, to stay still, but I was shaking uncontrollably and crying. Finally, one of the doctors told the technician to leave and come back at another time.

I had been alone at the time of the briefing, but my parents and twin sisters, Katie and Breidgeen, arrived shortly thereafter and tried to help me put what we could into perspective. After we had talked through the details of my situation, we moved on to a topic that they hoped would lift my spirits. I had always loved parties, so we began to plan a party for when I would be discharged from the hospital a few weeks later.

This party planning was a pivotal post-diagnosis moment. It not only gave me something to look forward to, but it was also my real first step in beginning to take the bull by the horns. Involving myself with the planning of an event for the future reminded me that I was still living. It got me to reframe my thinking to recognize that I was living with cancer, not dying from it.

If I was going to be living with cancer, I knew my health had to come first and foremost. It was going to take great strength to endure the medical regimen, so I made it my priority to do whatever I could to improve my health.

My cousin Michael called from California to tell me about different vitamins and minerals that he believed would be good for me. And he introduced me to visualization: I'd picture in my mind's eye white, purifying light cleansing the area where the tumor was. Or I'd visualize laser guns killing off the bad cells and replacing them with good cells. (I'll talk more about visualization techniques later in the book because I believe they made a huge difference in my recovery and my life thereafter.) Michael lost his mother, my Aunt Betty, to lung cancer when she was just fifty years old. Michael was a young man in his twenties at the time. I trust my cousin implicitly; moreover, knowing that he had gone through this with his mother made his advice that much more significant. Whenever I speak with other people going through some shipwreck-type situation, I always discuss visualization with them. I find it incredibly powerful, and I credit my cousin with empowering me with that knowledge.

Given the highly stressful circumstances—psychological, emotional, and physical—I needed to do what I could to minimize my stress as much as possible. I bought meditation tapes that helped me relax mentally and physically. *It was important for me to be really good to myself at that time.*

As my treatments, surgeries, and procedures continued, I decided I had two choices. Either I could go through life and draw whatever happiness I could from it, or I could be miserable. I chose happiness! I read in a self-help book (I wish I could remember the name of it) that the brain is like a muscle, and if I thought more pessimistic thoughts than positive ones, then when I had an idle moment my brain would always go to pessimism, and the opposite held true as well. I wanted to strengthen my brain with positive thoughts, so that when I had an idle moment it wouldn't be as bad. I began to recognize the importance of remaining aware and conscious of my thought process. Another self-help book I read during the treatments that I *do* remember the name of is *Full Catastrophe Living* by Jon Kabat-Zinn. It spoke about all of the various stressors in life (i.e., health stress, environmental stress, work stress, family stress, etc.) and how to handle them better. I ordered meditation and yoga tapes with an order form from the back of that book. The book and the tapes were tremendous helps to me, and I still refer to them from time to time.

After educating myself with books and speaking with as many people as possible, I realized I couldn't sustain the amount of misery I was experiencing and get through this experience intact. That led me to realize that I had a choice in how I handled things and perceived things. This isn't to say that from there on everything was great, but rather that I realized I had a choice in how I approached it. And, to the extent to which I had a choice, I was going to choose to be positive and optimistic.

Sure, there were plenty of times when the protocol got the best of me. Continuous spinal taps and bone marrow biopsies are just two examples of those times. During those times, I experienced a lot of mood swings that were either medically induced from the steroids or the chemo, or just stemmed from frustration and fear. One minute I felt incredibly angry and helpless. The next I felt positive and sure that the treatments would make me well again. Many times I was overwhelmed by the thought of death. Nevertheless, I tried my best to work through the emotions without repressing them, and get back on track with being positive and optimistic with regard to the final outcome—my cure.

There were times that my mind's eye did go to worst case scenarios; however, during those horrific visual moments, I would stop myself and say out loud, "Stop! Think only positive thoughts!" It wasn't easy. I had to force myself to think of happy things, like when the protocol would be over, when my hair would be back, and when I wouldn't need pain medication anymore because I would be completely healthy. It was forced at first, but then as time went on, those thoughts came more naturally. Yes, I was talking to myself, but that worked for me; I became less overwhelmed with horribly graphic mental visions.

It was crucial for me to work through my negative emotions instead of repressing them. I couldn't dwell on them, however, as it wouldn't have helped me at all. I learned through experience that when I tried to repress my negative emotions, my body rebelled, forcing me to deal with them in the form of anxiety attacks. I found that dealing with my feelings directly was crucial. And once I began to do it, my anxiety abated, my thoughts became clearer, and I found myself more able to keep my focus on that light at the end of the tunnel. A positive attitude was my best defense and offense.

One odd shift in perspective for me was that I eventually found myself thinking of cancer as a sort of vacation. I realize that for most people it is difficult, if not impossible, to associate the term "vacation" with the dreaded C word. Vacations are planned; cancer is not. Vacations are fun; cancer is not. But what they have in common is that they bring you out of your everyday life. They allow you the time and space to step back and reassess, and to open up to new experiences.

Cancer, certainly, was not the vacation I had always dreamed of. As I've said, vacations are usually planned and their objectives are typically fun, relaxation, and rejuvenation, not physical and emotional turmoil.

Post-diagnosis, my dream vacation was Hawaii. My plans ranged from what I would wear to the activities I've always wanted to do. During the planning stages, I enjoyed imagining the beautiful weather, the warm beach with calm waves, the scent of tropical flowers, the feel of trade winds, and the taste of fresh mahi-mahi. Watching the hula dancers around the pool and taking the sunset cruises were just a few of the activities I anticipated. In fact, I visualized every detail.

When I arrived three years after my protocol ended, on my honeymoon, it turned out to be better than I could have planned or even imagined. As I said earlier, pre-diagnosis I was not the kind of person to stop and smell the roses. But post-diagnosis, it was something I began to do, consciously realizing that it was one of the many things I took for granted. Hawaii was an amazing experience, and one that I truly believe I would not have enjoyed so intensely had I not had the experience of living with cancer.

Nevertheless, the planning and preparation did not necessarily mean that everything would turn out exactly the way I had envisioned. Life always manages to take surprising twists and turns no matter how much time I have to prepare. Sometimes a particular twist or turn along life's way can transform a well-planned vacation into an incredible adventure, or even transform a period of profound horror into an unimaginable vacation.

I was determined to overcome the devastating circumstances of my situation, and I was wholeheartedly dedicated to working my way back to good health. I began working harder and using all of my senses to keep myself in the "here and now" of each and every situation—to experience each moment to its fullest. I never felt more alive.

Despite being confined to the hospital for most of the first six months of my treatments, I was overcome with the desire to do things I had always wanted to do but had never made time for. And I saw no reason to wait until I was well. I was voracious for knowledge, particularly about my condition, so I learned everything I could from my hospital bed, reading about anatomy and physiology among other things, talking to people, and absorbing every learning experience possible.

The satisfaction this brought inspired me to take a bolder step. I had withdrawn from college after a semester and a half, but had always intended to go back and finish my degree. When I had first enrolled right out of high school, mainly at my parents' urgings, I hadn't quite been ready. Though I understood the importance of having a degree, I could not sufficiently apply myself. I had my sights set on other things.

I had always been especially close to my aunt, Rita McNulty, who was one of the first women traders on Wall Street, as far as my family knows. As a child, I had watched her ride around in limousines and travel the world, at a time when most working women were secretaries or teachers. When she had her first child, my cousin Meghan, the stock exchange announced it on the ticker tape. As we grew older, my aunt became my confidante and best friend, more like a sister than an aunt. And I wanted to follow in her footsteps.

Although after high school, I had initially gone along with my parents' wishes and given college a shot, what I really wanted was to work on Wall Street. As I'd watch the professors' lips move, I'd daydream about the glamour of the city, Wall Street, and all its glory. And soon, I withdrew from school. But after a few years on Wall Street, I came to realize that it wasn't as glamorous as I had imagined. I had the Series 7 and Series 63 licenses you need to trade stock, as well as an insurance license, and after spending time as a registered sales assistant I went on to become an account executive. But rather than feeling that my fantasies had been fulfilled, I found myself disillusioned. If anything, I found it repugnant. I worked in three different brokerage houses. The language was beyond atrocious; the brokers and traders sometimes hired strippers, when there was no escaping the view (short of putting my hands over my eyes or leaving the area); and men constantly wanted to cheat on their wives with me. These are just a few examples of what made my experience with Wall Street far from sensational. I still have the utmost respect for the stock market—the way it mirrors life with its unpredictable ups and downs—but my personal experience of working on Wall Street was unpleasant.

I will always be proud of my aunt and her achievements. It was a different time and she is an amazing lady. My encounter was entirely different than hers. While hers was glamorous, mine was just another one of life's many lessons.

I am a firm believer, though, in the sentiment "good comes out of bad," and I also believe everything happens for a reason. In my life, this is exemplified over and over again. One example of this is my withdrawing from college. I continued working full-time for six years. It was then, at age twenty-five, while working and living at home, that I was diagnosed. I filed for short-term disability through my employer, and Social Security began six months later. Social Security disability was long term, and after two years it was coupled with Medicare, which became my secondary insurance. If I had not worked full-time for at least a few years, I would not have been eligible for Social Security, which paid my bills while Medicare helped eliminate many of my medical costs. If I had finished my four years of college right out of high school I would not have had enough time in the workforce to accrue those financial benefits. It could have put my family in a financial crisis.

After about two months in the hospital bed, I realized this was the time for me to make a bold move: I enrolled in college classes again. Not knowing what to expect, I had a lot of anxiety about starting school again. I still had one hundred and twelve credits to go in order to earn my Bachelor's degree. It seemed like a large undertaking, but

I decided to take it day by day and see what happened—no pressure.

It helped that I had begun studying while I was in the hospital. It had put me in the proper mindset and started me thinking about what I wanted to focus on. I had aspirations to become either a physical therapist or a speech-language pathologist. Eventually, speech-language pathology became my vocational calling. Fortunately, during the following two years of my protocol, the treatments became less frequent, and I seized the opportunity.

My mother wanted to help me by taking the first couple of classes with me, which meant we'd have to take them at night after she came home from work. But I didn't care if it was morning, noon, or night; having her help me get through the initial stage of being back in a classroom, wearing a wig no less, alleviated a lot of the stress. My father, who also worked full-time, was a great help as well with my studying and in clarifying things when I was too tired or nauseous to comprehend.

The semester began in January, so it was cold and windy. I had a hooded scarf that I clenched at my throat so the hood wouldn't blow back and send my wig flying across the parking lot.

I started off taking one class. Before class began I introduced myself and my mother to the professor, and gave him a letter from my doctor explaining that my cancer might cause more than the allotted number of absences. I also had to ask not to be called on unless I raised my hand and not to be required to do the oral presentation listed on the syllabus. I was concerned that the painkillers, tranquilizers, and anti-nausea medication I was taking—along with my frequent exhaustion—would interfere with my ability to speak clearly and perform appropriately. I particularly didn't want to risk it in a room full of strangers. The professor looked concerned and assured me I had nothing to worry about.

I also let him know that it was extremely important to me that I earn my grade. I assured him that I'd write an extensive term paper in lieu of the oral speech, and that I'd study and research beyond the call of duty. Although I didn't *feel* any less intelligent from the surgeries, chemo, radiation, and all of the medication, I still had the need to prove my capability to myself and to confirm that I wasn't being given a free pass.

The professor agreed and told me what hours he had available if I needed extra help. My mother was so grateful; she looked as if she was going to cry.

Once we had taken our seats in the classroom, my mother looked at me and whispered, "The first class you had to pick was a four-credit anatomy and physiology class with a lab? Why not an art class? You know, start off slow and work our way up," she joked. My mother was an art history major, so that certainly would have made her life a lot easier.

I took one class with my mother for the first two semesters, which I found perfectly manageable. So, the following semester I signed up for two, this time on my own. But when my classes coincided with my chemotherapy treatments, it was much more challenging. When I was taking college courses while going for chemotherapy treatments, there were times when I knew I should only take one class, and there were other times when I knew I could handle a full load. It was a combination of my intense personal drive and my professors' faith in me that encouraged me to strive harder and forge ahead.

As time went on, I began to feel the pressure of time. I was older than most of the students, and I felt an increasing need to finish school faster. I remember thinking that every time I turned around I had another medical complication. For instance, I'd have an appointment for a chemo treatment and drive all the way into the city to Sloan-Kettering only to find out that I couldn't get my treatment because my blood count was not high enough, or I had a cold or virus of some kind. That meant I had to go back to Sloan-Kettering the following week, hoping my blood counts would be normal, along with everything else, so I could get the treatment. But inevitably the new appointment would be the only day the doctor had available, and it would happen to coincide with a mid-term or final exam.

My professors were extremely understanding of my situation and always did their best to help me; however, there was only so much they could do, and more than once I had to drop a class because of the conflicts between my protocol and school. Constantly revising and rescheduling my classes and appointments often seemed like a full-time job in and of itself. Psychologically, the pressure was mounting. I started to become extremely frustrated and upset. I wanted to finish school just as fast as I wanted to finish my protocol. That was pressure I was putting on myself and nothing good was coming out of it. I was totally stressing myself out!

Not having thought of getting a therapist at the time, and not knowing where to turn, I decided to speak with one of my professors to help organize my thoughts and get his input on what would be the best strategy under my circumstances. Quitting, I made it clear, was out of the question. My boyfriend (now my husband) Ronnie had a favorite expression, "Winners never quit and quitters never win," which I made my mantra. My professor summed up his response in one statement. *"It's not the amount of time it takes to work toward your goal that matters; it's the attainment of the goal that counts."* For me, at that time, his statement was somewhat profound. My professor reiterated something I knew all along, but had temporarily lost sight of: my main goal was getting healthy. The stress of time was becoming unhealthy for me.

It wasn't easy, and there were times I thought it would take forever to finish. But I settled down, paced myself, worked hard, and kept sight of my goals—getting well and finishing school, in that order.

I continued to go to school after my treatments ended, and

reached my goal when I received my Bachelor of Arts, specializing in speech-language pathology with a minor in psychology, from Hofstra University. It took five years from beginning to end, and although it was extremely difficult, the journey was worth every moment.

Another aspect of this "new beginning" perk is that it allowed me to do things at my own pace—a pace that suited my needs. That in itself was a stress reducer. How often do we get the chance to set our own pace? We live in a world of time frames and deadlines, and are bombarded by expectations and demands. Now, I got to take that deep breath and that big step back. I took a good, long, hard look at the big picture—the panoramic view—to see what was rushing me through life.

As time went on there were days, even weeks, when I did not feel like doing anything at all. My body was telling me to rest and take it easy. That reality had to be met with compliance. *During those periods of low energy, I realized that it was all right to feel that way, and that my fatigue was only temporary.* It did not hold me back, however, from setting and achieving my goals. True health requires both a healthy body and a positive mind. As time passed, I realized it was all up to me. As I took charge of my life, it became increasingly a time of joy, rest, and renewal—ideal circumstances for a new beginning.

Perk 2
Finding Care-givers Everywhere

I tried to surround myself with people who I believed cared about me and would be good to me throughout my ordeal. I was fortunate in that my family, friends, medical team—and often even strangers—were a constant source of love, encouragement, and assistance. The support and camaraderie of other cancer patients were just as important. Although our experiences were personal and unique, we'd all experienced things that only a fellow patient could relate to, such as the piercing reality of going day by day confronting our own mortality.

Someone once asked me if I felt like I was in a sort of club when I saw someone going through something similar. The answer is yes. But I wouldn't define it as a club, *per se*—more like a mutual understanding. Only those who have stared death in the face and have either survived or are still struggling with the disease really get what a fellow patient is going through. When someone asked me what it was like, the only way I knew how to describe it was to compare it to when someone is planning a wedding or having a baby. For many people, until you do it yourself you do not and cannot fully understand what that person went through or is going through.

I'm comparing apples and oranges, but again this is the only way I know how to describe it. I didn't know what it was like to have children when my cousin Patti (who is two months younger than me) had her first child. Patti and I are very close, more like sisters than cousins, but when she married and then had a baby ten months later, it seemed as if we had a lot less to talk about. I was still living for the weekends, so I couldn't appreciate how difficult it was to raise a child until I had my own seven years later. I was only able to *imagine* the difficulty. For me, it's the same thing with cancer.

In the beginning, it seemed like one big waiting game. Actually, the old saying, "hurry up and wait," was more to the point. I rushed to doctors' offices, laboratories, radiology centers, nuclear medicine centers, and so on to have tests done. I wanted answers immediately. All of my unanswered questions became more and more frightening. But everything took time. I realized how many holidays there were in a year, as I had to wait that extra day or, even worse, the three-day weekend. At those times, patience really was a virtue. I tried to keep myself busy, hoping to pass the time and take my mind off what was really going on. I enjoy golf, so when I was up to it I went to the driving range and hit buckets of balls. I read a lot of self-help books, took long walks, and went out with my friends as well.

When I was initially admitted to Sloan-Kettering, I remember sitting on my hospital bed praying to my Aunt Betty. She had passed away of cancer five years before I ended up with the same horrific diagnosis, only hers was lung cancer and mine was lymphoma. I knew she understood how I was feeling. The words fear, trepidation, and apprehension did not begin to describe it. The terror of the unknown when confronting my mortality and the ultimate consequences of what was at stake were unbearable. The thought of the possible pain of loss—the loss of my life and those I loved—and the hurt for those who would be in pain over losing me was overwhelming.

As I prayed to Aunt Betty for strength, guidance, and some understanding of why this was happening, I felt a rush go through my body. Quite honestly, I cannot put the feeling into words. It was as if some sort of energy surged through me. Out loud I said, "That was strange. Was that you, Aunt Betty?" I went on thinking, *Are you with me? Did you send someone down to be with me to help get me through this?* All I knew was from that moment on I did not feel as if I was going through my diagnosis and protocol alone. I felt as if there was a presence with me, or a presence that went through me, making me stronger than before. In that moment—and it only lasted for a moment—I felt peace, comfort, and tranquility.

Needless to say, those feelings came and went just as the fear and everything that came with it managed to come and go as well. It was just an experience that I will never forget. I feel, in addition to being diagnosed with cancer, that as a result of my "Aunt Betty moment," my life was altered forever. It was and will always be indescribable and unforgettable.

During those trying times, my recognition of a kind world in general was a revelation as well. Family, friends, professors, co-workers, acquaintances, and even strangers were willing to listen. They are just a few examples of my faithful support. Believe it or not, salespeople were even willing to forgo commissions due them on purchases I made. It was absolutely incredible. Once, I went to a well-known furniture store to purchase a day bed. After the sale was completed, the kind salesman called another department regarding the delivery. There was an eighty-five dollar delivery charge. As the salesman and I waited for the return phone call, we engaged in small talk. He inquired as to what I did for a living, so I told him that I was out on disability and why. He jumped up out of his chair, went through the paperwork, and asked me why I did not inform him of this earlier. He reduced the purchase price of the bed by thirty percent and made sure the delivery was free. In addition, he wanted me to call him within a few months to let him know how I was doing. How incredibly kindhearted was that!

Pre-diagnosis, I had grown up to be a cautious person, and with good reason. Here are a few examples:

In 1978, when I was twelve and living in Brooklyn, my friend and I were walking around the neighborhood one summer night, which was something my parents never permitted. We were a few blocks away from home, and to make a long story short, a car tried to run us down. The driver backed up and tried twice. My friend and I ran through backyards, hopping fences, to make our way home.

We moved to Garden City, Long Island, in 1982 (about forty-five minutes from Manhattan) when I was sixteen years old. In 1987, when I was twenty-one, I was on my way home from a seminar to help me pass the exam for my Series 7 stockbrokers' license. I was on 33rd Street heading toward Penn Station at eight o'clock in the evening on a cold, rainy night. A tall man grabbed my breast and wouldn't let go. Within a matter of seconds, thousands of images flashed before my eyes. I feared he might force me into the alley between two stores that was right next to us. I was terrified of rape and every other horrifying image that appeared in my mind's eye. The guy's hold on me seemed to last for a very long time—too long. He set my adrenaline into full motion. I began to scream at the top of my lungs, and beat him to the point where he ran. He *tried* to grab my bag before running but, at that point, I wasn't giving up *anything!* I had no idea where my strength came from—all I knew was that I sent the mugger running for his life. As he flew down 33rd Street, I continued to scream, "Get back here, I'm not done with you yet!" What was I thinking! I cried all the way home on the train to Garden City.

Those were just a few of the experiences that weakened my faith in mankind. I was always the kind of person who was very trusting, caring, giving, and genuinely interested in the well-being of others. But I also developed extremely protective, defensive, and overly cautious attributes. At the time they seemed necessary in life. However, that is not so! Don't get me wrong. I believe it is wise for me to be protective, defensive and cautious, as long as it is proportionate. Anything done to an extreme, I believe, is unhealthy, regardless of what it is.

The cancer diagnosis was the worst thing that had ever happened to me, but at the same time it brought me hope—the eye-opening recollection and recognition of a kind world. I began to see people differently. My once cynical ways were put aside because there was no room for them anymore. The outpouring of goodwill from everyone around me was so overwhelming; it had to be embraced wholeheartedly.

The good now outweighed the bad tenfold. Most people no longer took advantage, and the negative element of society did not have the chance to demolish my faith in people altogether. It was the good that always prevailed. The big picture became very clear. I wanted to stay focused on the positive, and I wanted to stay in touch with the kind world.

But even in a kind world, the word "cancer" is hard for most people to handle. For example, my mother has the talent of going into denial as a defense mechanism. As I stated in the last chapter, she was always supportive and her love for me was never in question. However, there's an ongoing joke, even pre-cancer, about my mother being the queen of denial (and they're not talking about the river). My mother has a unique way of going into someone's hospital room, including mine, grasping her own cheeks, opening her eyes wide, and—in her Brooklyn accent— telling the patient, family, or friend, "Oh, my God! You look awful. I can't believe it, you look awful!" There have been times when Mom has been escorted out of friends' hospital rooms. But then, once she arrived home, she went right back into denial mode. Although denial helped my mother cope, at times it was quite frustrating for me. But I also had to understand that my situation was a difficult time for everyone. I did my best to try to protect loved ones from the physical and mental pain I was experiencing while fighting for my life.

My father tended to be more level-headed and less dramatic with his visits to family and friends in the hospital. But it was hard for him to hide his emotions when it came to me. With each visit, I could see in his eyes the pain of seeing me in that condition, and I could sense the helplessness he felt because he couldn't end my suffering.

For the first six months of my protocol, my sisters, Katie and Breidgeen, had to drive me everywhere—I was not allowed to drive because of the medications I was taking. For whatever reason, the chemo made me crave soft ice cream with melted marshmallow, hot fudge, and whipped cream. That, or the spiciest of the spicy buffalo wings—it went from one extreme to the other. But they were real cravings. So, every night one of my sisters was either running to get me the ice cream de jour or the hot and spicy wings. That helped to contribute to the quality of my life.

It was interesting to see how each of my friends reacted when they found out that I had cancer. Some were concerned that my hair would fall out, others were afraid I would not be able to partake in happy hour with a few cocktails, and still others were desperately saddened that I had to go through a rigorous protocol. Whenever we went out, they made sure to take care of me—if I needed to sit down, they brought me a chair. If I needed my medication, and it was out in the car, they went to get it for me. They all went out of their way to make sure I was doing all right.

When I was in the hospital, my friend Barbara laid down in the bed with me and kept me company. Just knowing she was there eliminated the fear and confusion that consumed my mind and body.

Another time, my cousin Timmy walked into my hospital room. He was one step away from being bald. I said, "Hi, Timmy. Did you shave your head for me?" At the time I was on all sorts of medication and thinking, *He is so cool to have shaved his head so I wouldn't have to be the only bald cousin.* I was twenty-five and the oldest cousin. No one else was bald. Timmy was twenty-one at the time. We had so many laughs during his visit with me—something I desperately needed.

My friend Jean and I were in the ladies' room at a local bar one night fixing our makeup, and at her request I took off my wig to show her what was underneath. She was the first friend to see my bald head, and the reaction I received was quite comforting. She was not shocked or repelled at all. It was almost as if she was saying, "So what, you're still Erin." It was because of her that I became comfortable keeping my wig off at home. Before then, I was afraid someone might come to the front door and pass out from shock just by looking at me.

Normally I was upset about being bald. However, when my friend Kristin called or came over to the house to see me, I ended up laughing uncontrollably. She managed to say outrageously funny things to me about how I wore my wigs and how I looked bald. Kristin is one of the most quick-witted people I know, and only she would be able to get away with saying the things that she said. For me to be able to laugh about being bald and having to wear a wig was a great gift from a great friend.

One of the times I was out in the Hamptons, I was having a few problems eating as a result of the chemotherapy. My friend Donna and I have been friends since we were three years old. She was trying her best to encourage me to ingest even the smallest morsel of food. I had lost about twenty pounds at that time, leaving me at about one hundred and twenty pounds. I'm five feet eight inches tall, and always weighed around one hundred and forty-five pounds—which was the perfect, healthy weight for me. I was always able to hide twenty pounds on the up-side and on the down-side with the right clothes, but anything below that made me *look* sick.

Donna and I were having lunch and I could not eat the macaroni and cheese. This was highly unusual for me. Donna sat there crying, begging me to eat, but it was impossible. Donna always made me laugh with her incredible sense of humor, and there she was crying. It broke my heart to see her so upset, yet at the same time I appreciated her concern. I knew the only way I could help make her feel better was to take her to happy hour, so off we went.

I feel very blessed to have had the support of my family and friends that I needed to get me through that tumultuous time in my life.

I took for granted how fortunate I was until one day, in the treatment center, a woman told us fellow chemo patients about how she had to take the train to and from Sloan-Kettering for her treatments. She said that after she was diagnosed, one by one, her family and friends stopped calling, to the point where she told us she felt so alone. She cried as she told us about her experience, and I cried too, along with everyone else in the room. It was her last treatment and she reported that she was doing very well medically. I hope she went on with her life, healthy, and found new friends who truly care about her. It made me realize how lucky I was.

The revelation brought about a change in spirit, which renewed my ability to be more thankful for family and friends. This transition was one of the most encouraging aspects of my life. Doors, once subconsciously closed, swung wide open, and I could now see my family and friends in the light of day. Other doors just kept opening and opening within me, almost to the point where my heart flooded with all of these indescribable emotions and feelings that were so completely positive and healthy. Throughout my illness, my relationships with family and friends became more intense, more united. I consider that to be a major perk!

The doctor-patient relationship is extremely intimate as well. It takes time to develop, but it took me a while to realize this. According to most individuals, doctors have the power to decide whether we will live or die. How intense! This is true to some degree. By using medical technology in conjunction with their wealth of medical knowledge, doctors are, by far, the most qualified to make that judgment call. Doctors are unique and caring human beings who have made the admirable career choice to help the sick. But even though I have always had, and still have, the utmost respect and appreciation for the medical profession, I believe that it is God who ultimately decides whether we will live or die, not doctors.

I knew I was in for the fight of my life, and I developed a fierce determination to defy the charted statistics. Cancer forced me to don my armor and unsheathe my sword—I declared war! I needed courage to be my constant companion. Courage was something I always knew I had but never realized to what degree. Once I drew on it, I reached a better understanding of its depth. It was my seemingly unlimited reservoir of fortitude that carried me through the worst of times.

I needed to develop confidence in my doctor so I would be able to open up and discuss anything and everything, no matter how insignificant I thought it might be. *I came to realize there was no such thing as an insignificant statement, question, or concern.* They were all very significant. If I did not ask the questions or clarify my thoughts, the doctor would not have been able to help me one hundred percent.

Furthermore, I found that it was essential for me to offer as much information as possible to the doctor during an evaluation. This held true for the case history as well. I could not omit any information out of fear or embarrassment.

As time progressed, I became more and more comfortable with my doctors. As a result of having them know me inside and out, my doctors also knew my joys (when I heard good news about how the tumor was shrinking), hopes (one day I'll go on to have a healthy life), fears (the treatment and surgeries could make me permanently disabled, and possibly be the cause of me never having a family of my own), and weaknesses (the feeling I sometimes had of the grim reaper hanging over my shoulder).

I was honest with my doctors, and they were honest with me—too honest at times. I had no desire to hear the risks, but due to the nature of their job they had to tell me. If I was receiving a particular treatment or going to have surgery, the doctor had to tell me each and every associated risk factor. Although it was prudent, I did not necessarily appreciate it. It had reached the point where even if the risk factor was one in a trillion, they were obliged to inform me. They were usually extremely frank when providing the risk factors, and at times did not understand why I became upset.

I will never forget the time, just two months into my treatments, when my mother and I were being informed about a surgery I had to have on my head. My cancer could have spread to my brain, so they treated me prophylactically with chemotherapy. Using spinal taps, the doctor took out cerebral spinal fluid to test, and then injected chemotherapy back into my spine. However, my spine built up fatty tissue as a defense, so the spinal taps were no longer working. The doctors had to implant an Ommaya shunt into my brain so they could treat the brain directly. As my mother and I sat for the briefing on how this procedure would take place, the doctor informed us that this surgery was quite common, and he did many of them every week. We found that reassuring. But then he went on to say that the day before the surgery they were going to introduce a current of air up my spine via a spinal tap and sonogram, which would open the ventricle in my brain. The doctors, technicians, and nurses told me I might experience a headache after the procedure. I pictured my headache would be something similar to a stress headache or maybe even my worst hangover. Neither of the above applied. I did not experience a headache. Rather, I felt as if my head was going to explode. I was screaming for morphine. I had not experienced anything as strong as morphine yet during the whole cancer ordeal, but I was not going to wait to see if the other "painkillers" were strong enough to get rid of the pain. The doctor went on to describe the surgery to my mother and me. He informed us he was going to cut open my scalp, drill a hole in my skull, and insert a catheter into the now inflated ventricle in my brain. The bad news—I couldn't even go there. The good news was that I would be under general anesthesia the whole time and I would not remember a thing. That I was able to deal with.

Next, the doctor informed my mother and me about the risks involved. He told us I could go blind or have brain damage. There were many other risk factors involved that I am sure he informed us about, but once I'd heard those two I only heard "la la la" after that.

Sometimes the mind can only take in so much, and this doctor was pressing my limits. My mother and I started crying. I just kept saying, "Oh my God, oh my God." The doctor looked at us as if we were two overly sensitive individuals. Maybe many people could stand that sort of encounter and come through it unscathed. But I seriously doubt it. Thankfully, I was completely knocked out for the whole surgery and the recovery was surprisingly quick. The doctor did an excellent job.

The surgery did not decrease my intellectual capacity at all, nor did it affect my 20/20 vision. What the surgery did, though, was give me a profound appreciation for my intellect and perfect vision, things I had always taken for granted.

Not only were my doctor–patient relationships intimate, but they took time to develop. My relationship with my oncologist went through many phases. It started off as nervous trust. I had no idea what was going on. However, I heard he was the best in his field and came highly recommended. Once I met with him, he was reassuring and exuded professional confidence. I was certain he would cure me. I wouldn't allow myself to think otherwise; the alternative was way too frightening.

But as time went on I began to develop resentment toward his unsympathetic attitude. For example, one time the wait in the waiting room was so long—hours—that Aunt Rita came with me into the exam room to give the doctor a piece of her mind.

"How could you keep this girl waiting so long when you know she needs a spinal tap and results from her bone marrow biopsy?" she asked, as mad as mad could be. "I mean, really, who do you think you are to ... " She tried to continue, but the doctor cut her off.

"You need to step outside now," the doctor said in a tone that made it clear that he was not going to deal with my aunt.

"But, but ... ," she continued as the door closed behind her.

"How dare you talk to my Aunt Rita that way!" I roared. "She loves me, and she's concerned. Don't ever talk to her like that again! Now let's get this over with," I said, then proceeded to put my headphones on. The procedure took about fifteen minutes from beginning to end, so listening to music while getting spinal taps was something I did every time.

During the spinal tap, the doctor would take out cerebral spinal fluid to biopsy, and then inject chemotherapy—the prophylactic treatment to the brain. I would put the headphones on, turn on my favorite radio station loudly, and tune out what was going on. It wasn't as if I wasn't dealing with what was going on. I understood the significance; however, that was *my* way of dealing. For whatever reason, the distraction made it easier and less painful for me.

On the way home Aunt Rita said, "I really regret yelling at the doctor like that. Was he gentle with you?" she asked. She looked upset.

"Aunt Rita, you have nothing to worry about," I said. "He was neither better nor worse. It's not like going to a restaurant and going off on the waiter or waitress shouting how bad the food is, demanding it be sent back to be fixed, and then having to worry about them spitting in the food."

We both laughed and went home relieved that it was another treatment checked off the list, and happy there weren't any negative reports from prior tests.

Regardless of the fact that my oncologist's bedside manner did not give me the warm and fuzzies, I would rather have an oncologist who is great at what he does professionally, but lacks bedside manner than one who has terrific bedside manner, but is professionally incompetent. After giving it some thought, I began to imagine what it would be like in his shoes, and I realized that he may have desensitized himself because he witnesses patients dying every day. This was a hospital filled only with cancer patients. The patients ranged from early stage to terminal. I feel that would toughen anyone up.

As time went on, though, throughout all of the stages of our relationship—the good, the bad, and the ugly, not necessarily in that order—we progressed to the point where I feel love and appreciation for my oncologist and his caring treatment, which culminated in a cure. I was fortunate because my oncologist, in my opinion, was the best in so many ways. He became one of the most important people in my life, and he will always have a special place in my heart.

When my protocol ended, I gave him a crystal clock. I wrote a letter to go with it explaining that the clock represented how the time passes, no matter what. During the treatments he continuously reassured me that one day the treatments would end. It was hard to digest that at first because it seemed like such a large chunk of my life was being wasted. However, as time went on my perspective changed. He thanked me, sent me a very thoughtful thank-you letter, and still has the clock on his desk to this day.

My oncologist and his wife shared in my wedding day three years after my chemotherapy treatments ended. And, even though the doctors thought it would take a miracle for me to have children, I did just that. So much for the predicted menopause after treatments! Four years after my treatments ended I had my first child. Ronnie and I brought each new baby to the oncologist's office so my children could meet the man who made it possible that we are all here. The smile that lit up his face every time was priceless.

On another note, just as I believe that my oncologist saved me from my bout with cancer, I believe my internist saved my life over and over again after treatments. In addition, she and I had something in common.

When I was seven years old, my family moved from one part of Brooklyn, called the Junction, because individuals started to deal drugs around our neighborhood. We moved up Flatbush Avenue to a different part of Brooklyn called Marine Park. I missed my two best friends, Donna and William. But we remained in touch, and I adapted. My pediatrician remained the same after our move. Actually, he remained my pediatrician up until my family had to move again nine years later from Brooklyn to Long Island, when I was sixteen.

I went from attending an all-girls Catholic school for ten years, taking mass transportation everywhere, including elementary school and my first two years of high school, to Garden City, New York (Long Island). It was there that I finished my junior and senior years in a public school, with boys in my class, having to wear a different outfit every day, and taking a school bus for the first time in my life. For me, the uniform was *so* much easier, and at the time I didn't think the school bus was cool at all. It wasn't easy, but once again, I adapted. Thankfully, I obtained my driver's license during my first year on Long Island, and I was able to merge my Brooklyn friends with my newfound Garden City friends.

After the move, I no longer had a pediatrician, an internist, or a family doctor. If we needed a doctor of some kind, my parents would take turns flipping through the GHI book to find a doctor that was close by. That seemed fine at the time. However, I've learned that my heath is only as good as my doctor.

My friend Barbara introduced me to her internist after having to listen to me tell her about all of the medical problems I was running into post-chemo.

When I first met the internist there was something very familiar about her. Even though I met her when I was twenty-eight, I felt as if I had known her all my life. I believe people are put in my life for certain reasons.

When we finished getting my medical history down in the

internist's notes, we went into the exam room and started to make small talk. I was asking her questions like, "What made you decide you wanted to become a doctor?"

With a big grin, she responded, "My father was a surgeon. When we were kids, he studied under a wonderful man who owned a beautiful home with an office in Brooklyn." She continued, "It was a brownstone and when you opened the door to the office, chimes would ring. He was my pediatrician."

Feeling like that was way too familiar, I asked, "Did he have nice leather couches and a grand piano in the waiting room?"

"Yes! How did you know that?" she asked.

"Did he also live with his sister and have a brother who sold shoes?" I asked, beginning to realize her pediatrician was mine as well.

"Dr. Jennings?" she said.

"Yes! I can't believe you and I had the same pediatrician, and in Brooklyn no less," I responded, just as shocked as she appeared to be. "Dr. Jennings was my mother's pediatrician. That's why we went to him."

My internist was about twenty years older than me—closer to my mother's age. We spent some time talking about what a great doctor he was. What a small world!

Before long, my internist became my anchor, essential to the quality of my life. Within just a few months I had drug-induced hepatitis resulting in abnormal liver function, a benign mass in my breast that was surgically removed, gastrointestinal difficulties that required endoscopic procedures, a possible cyst on my pituitary gland that required endocrinological studies and extensive followup with continuous MRIs due to the Ommaya shunt implanted in my brain, and so much more. The specialists, to whom I was referred by my internist, consisted of a gastroenterologist, a breast specialist, a neurologist, and an endocrinologist, to name a few. As these doctors treated me, they reported back to my internist. In turn, she explained in detail everything that was happening to me and what would be done about it. If there was something I did not understand, she clarified it for me. In my opinion, my internist is brilliant and one of the strongest people I have ever met. She has since retired. What a loss to the medical profession and her patients. She not only dedicated her life to medicine—she genuinely cares very deeply for each of her patients.

There were times when she stayed on the phone with me for hours, either comforting or encouraging me in some way. It was as if she became my mentor. At that point in my life, right after I was finished with the protocol and was ready to continue on with my life, my internist convinced me I was able to do anything and everything I put my mind to. She made me feel that there were no limits to what I was capable of accomplishing. She was right. My medical conditions never held me back from doing whatever I chose to do. My internist demonstrated unique professional and personal skills, and as a result I look upon her with great admiration and appreciation.

I must say, with regard to my medical care, the relationship between my caregivers and me was extremely profound. Having cancer and being cared for in a hospital or a doctor's office was way beyond a business relationship or money matter. Moreover, we were a partnership of professionals—they were the professional medical providers and I was the professional patient. All were considered full-time jobs. The relationship was not based on purely monetary or material considerations. True, fees and costs were a reality. But the real nature of the "care transaction" was, at its core, wholly human and even spiritual. It is comforting to know that in this so-called veil of tears however many mistakes are made or judgments falter, we encounter along the way good and caring souls who are truly dedicated to alleviating the suffering of others and healing them when the body breaks. I have been fortunate to encounter many such souls during my siege by cancer.

Perk 3
Breaking out of the Cosmetic Rut

When I was first diagnosed, I thought my life was going to be put on hold. But I was wrong. My life changed for the better in ways that I could not have ever imagined. I spoke with many individuals—men and women—who experienced the same revelation. They had all thought their significant others, or even friends and family, would have been taken aback or repelled by their physical appearance.

My hair was a significant part of my personality. It made a statement about who I was and how I was feeling. For example, I would put my hair up in a ponytail, subtly signifying my casual mood. On special occasions, when I wanted to feel especially attractive, I spent more time ensuring that my hair looked just right. These little rituals became a major part of my life without my even realizing it.

Before losing my hair, I had a particular look that I favored for years—too many years—and had great reluctance deviating from it. It was auburn, wavy, and halfway down my back. If I wanted it curly,

I used gel, crunched it, and used a diffuser. If I wanted it straight, I just blew it straight. My reluctance was a fear of change, and it became so intimidating that I refused to change my hairstyle with the times. My '80s hairstyle that looked great in the eighties looked completely outdated in the early '90s. It looked as if I was in a cosmetic rut.

Cancer and chemotherapy brought about change, by no choice of my own. As most of my chemotherapy treatments resulted in hair loss, they brought about tremendous emotional upheaval as well. All of a sudden, my identity was in question. Who was this person I saw in the mirror? Would people still love me? Might I frighten them? As superficial as that may seem, it was a reality for me. That identity crisis was the furthest thing from superficial. As a woman, not only did it seem unnatural to be completely hairless, but it was a constant reminder of the disease.

When I was first diagnosed and informed that my hair would fall out, I panicked. *Where do I go for a wig? What type of hair do I get? What if it looks terrible?* In the beginning, I had a few weeks before the hair loss took place, so I shopped around. I went to shopping malls and tried on a few wigs. I was horrified! They all looked like the kind of wigs I would wear on Halloween. At that point, I thought it was hopeless. I was doomed to stand out as a person who was obviously wearing a wig. That was the last thing in the world that I wanted, because an obvious wig would bring questions. I did not want to deal with the onslaught of questions because I felt my personal life was just that—personal! If I wanted someone to know I was sick, I would tell them myself, as opposed to being put in the position of having to tell people just because I was wearing a hideous wig. I searched high and low for the perfect wig. Then one day it happened. I found a wig store about three miles from my house that not only sold wigs but actually provided a complete wig service. They trimmed the wigs to my liking, washed them for me when needed and much more. This store employed individuals who were professional, considerate of my feelings, understanding of my situation, and compassionate. They made my horrible ordeal somewhat tolerable. I tried on a few different styles. There were some that made me look like I needed a complete makeover. The funny thing is that before the chemo I really did need a serious makeover. Fortunately, there were others that looked great. They looked like real hair and were inexpensive. My prayers were answered!

Most insurance companies cover the purchase of a wig under these circumstances. I am a natural redhead and there were wigs there that matched my hair completely, texture and all, and the cost was only one hundred and thirty-five dollars. My insurance company covered one, and once I felt more confident, I purchased several others for fun. In total, I bought a platinum blonde, a long brunette, a short brunette, and two red wigs. In the beginning, I wore all of them at different times to different places; however, after a while, I tended only to wear the one I liked best. That was the one that matched my natural hair most closely. Thankfully, I bought two of them. One became my weekday wig, enduring a lot of wear and tear, and the other became my weekend wig. When one was being cleaned, I always had the other as a backup.

Even though I came to love my wigs, there were a few uncomfortable moments because I didn't wear them at all times. One situation occurred early in the protocol, when my friend Vicki and her mom, Marie, came to visit me in the hospital. Vicki and I have been friends since we were about thirteen, and her family always treated me as if I was one of their own. Vicki and I went through the teenage years right up into adulthood together. As I watched both of them look into my room, look at me, and keep walking, I realized they did not recognize me. I wondered, *Do they see me the same way I saw everyone in the hospital when I first arrived?* To me everyone looked the same—bald and confused.

I called out, "Hi guys. I'm in here. Vicki, Marie, I'm over here." As they backtracked into my room, Vicki said she didn't recognize me without my hair. When we were kids, Vicki and I were very much into our hair, and Marie would pretend I was her student or client when she was a hairdresser. We had great fun with it. So, to lighten the mood, I pointed to my head and said jokingly, "Okay, it's a little different than before, but, Marie, I'm sure we can work with it. What do you think?"

They both smiled and gave me a present. It was a St. Jude medal on a beautiful chain. I thanked them for their thoughtful gift and we spent a nice afternoon together. After they left, I held the medal and continuously prayed to St. Jude for my health.

Throughout the ordeal, I knew my health came first, and as time went on I slowly began to grasp that the hair issue was not a medical problem but a cosmetic one. Nonetheless, mentally, it was painful to look in the mirror and have a stranger staring back. I expected the professionals in the hospital to appreciate this pain and act accordingly. Some did, but there were a few times when the doctors and nurses forewarned me about my pending hair loss in a monotone voice. It sounded something like they were sorry to have to inform me, but I was about to receive one of the chemo treatments that would make all of my hair fall out. They would insist that I have a wig ready for use.

During this personal experience, my hair fell out five times due to two and a half years of chemotherapy. The first time was during the induction phase of my protocol. My hair fell out three weeks after my treatments began, and I remained bald for at least six months, eyelashes, eyebrows, nose hair, and all. Then I had eighteen radiation treatments in one month, followed by the two-year maintenance phase of my protocol. My maintenance phase was made up of a three-month program that was repeated over and over. I received a significant amount of chemotherapy in each three-month cycle, most of which did not cause hair loss. However, two of the chemo agents were only given to me in alternate cycles (that is, every six months instead of every three), and one of them—Adriamycin—caused the hair loss. So, for two years, my hair fell out every six months, and then started to grow back again. I would manage to grow it back into a cute, short hairstyle, and then they would give me the Adriamycin again and it would all fall out. Every time it happened, I thought, *Come on. I just got used to not having to wear that uncomfortable thing!*

The first time my hair began to fall out, I was in the shower. As I shampooed, clumps of wet red hair wrapped themselves all over my hands and arms, clinging to my face and blinding me with disgust. The horror I felt was indescribable. It was as if I was covered with bugs from which I tried desperately to escape. But the hair continued to come out of my scalp, enveloping my entire body. I scrubbed my arms, smacked my legs, and tried to rip the hair that was once in my head off my body. It was a losing battle. I eventually had to come out of the shower, dry off, and let the hair naturally fall off me as I screamed, cried, and punched walls. That went on for days. Even though I was told what to expect, I was not prepared.

However, I learned a lot from that first hair-loss experience. It was always traumatic, but nevertheless I became more equipped for handling the second, and future, occurrences. The first time, I continuously brushed my hair for days until it stopped falling out. What a mess—the floors, the sheets, everywhere I looked there was hair.

As I mentally prepared for my hair to fall out again, I developed a technique. From then on, whenever my hair was to fall out, I put the radio on to my favorite station—playing nice and loud—opened a brown paper bag from the supermarket, and sat down in a chair with the bag at my feet. I then proceeded to put my head between my legs and over the bag. When I was finally situated, I pulled the loose hair out and it fell directly into the bag. There was no mess to clean up, and after I finished pulling out the loose hair, I removed whatever little was left with a barber's buzzer that I bought at a department store. This gave me a sense of control as opposed to feeling like a helpless victim. I was the one removing the hair from my scalp, and I was in charge of how the process took place. The process no longer had control over me. That alleviated a lot of terror and confusion. It took about half an hour from beginning to end, as opposed to days of pure torture.

Being bald and having to wear a wig was a harrowing experience, but it was also an amazing experience. One time, when I was in a public restroom, a woman I had never met before sang the praises of my newly found investment.

She said, "I love your hair. Would you mind giving me the name and number of whoever does it?"

"You can't afford this hairdo," I said, smiling.

"Excuse me?" she said.

"No, no, no, I have cancer and I'm going for chemo treatments. This is a wig," I said, still smiling. "My medical bills are outrageous, that's all I meant." I never wanted anyone to pity me. That's why I always kept a smile on my face when discussing the cancer. I didn't think there was a need to make anyone feel uncomfortable, or afraid of putting their foot in their mouth.

"You have a great attitude," she said. "I saw you with your friends hanging out by the bar, laughing and having fun. I think I'd be in my room every night if I were going through what you're going through. I hope to see you again soon," she said as she left the ladies' room.

That acclamation continually came from people who had no idea I was wearing a wig. They all thought it was my natural hair. I received more compliments on my wig than I had ever received on my natural hair. It was absolutely unbelievable. Men asked me out on dates having no idea I was sick. As a matter of fact, when I met my husband nine months into my protocol, he did not know I was sick and wearing a wig. I didn't feel the need to tell anyone and everyone who mentioned my hair that it was a wig. That was my business. There were times, though, when I was left with no other choice.

An example of this was when I was up in Hunter Mountain, New York, in a bar called HVI. I always spoke with whomever was standing around me. There was one night when I was forced to tell a guy that I had cancer and I was wearing a wig. He kept touching it and trying to twirl my hair—uugghh!

"Could you stop playing with my hair, please?" I asked.

"Why? I like it," he said.

"I don't, so please stop."

"Oh, are you one of those girls who doesn't like having your hair messed up?" he asked sarcastically. For some reason, the more I pleaded that he stop touching my hair, the more he wanted to. I walked to a different area over and over trying to get away from him. Even my friends told him to leave me alone, but he was persistent—or should I say annoying. Eventually I had to tell him the truth.

"I have cancer and this is a wig," I said pointing to my head. "Could you please stop following me, you're making me really uncomfortable."

"You do not have cancer," he said.

"Yeah, I do," I said.

He began to look confused and embarrassed. He said, "How do I know you're telling me the truth? I just wanted to talk to you, not upset you."

I saw something in that guy's eyes that made me feel like I could prove it to him and he wouldn't humiliate me. I took a chance and held his hand, brought it up to my neck, and let him feel the netting at the base of the wig where it met my neck.

"Oh my God, you're telling the truth. No wonder your friends were furious with me. They kept telling me to leave you alone. How come they didn't tell me why?" he asked as he placed his hand on my arm.

"They know that I don't want them telling anyone. If I wanted someone to know, I'd tell them myself."

"I'm so sorry. Now I'm buying you your drinks all night," he said.

"Get out of here!" I said laughing. "Just stop following me around. Deal?" I said with a smile, trying to let him know that everything was okay. I didn't want him to follow me around, nor did I want him to feel like garbage. Luckily, it ended amicably.

In addition to my hair, another form of significant cosmetic change was makeup. Pre-cancer, it was usually essential for me. I have that fair Irish skin, with fair eyelashes and eyebrows—a complete facial washout. Because makeup was necessary most of the time, I could have applied it blindfolded. I had been using the same application for years. I started with the foundation and then the powder. I then moved on to the eyebrows, eyelids, eyeliner, mascara, blush, and the grand finale was the lipstick. It was the same thing every day. My mechanical and somewhat monotonous application was another little ritual that had become a major part of my life without my even realizing it. During the day, my makeup application was light and casual, whereas at night, for parties or functions, the application became more dramatic. I knew how to work my makeup so it was appropriate for whatever was on the social calendar.

However, once I began chemotherapy, my mechanical and somewhat monotonous application had to be altered. My complexion became pale, grayish, and somewhat blotchy. In addition to that, my eyelashes and eyebrows fell out. I was fortunate that my wig had bangs, which concealed my lack of eyebrows, although all I needed was an eyebrow liner and I was set. Foundation and blush took care of my pale, blotched complexion. The only major problem was the absence of eyelashes. After some trial and error, I compensated with very dark eyeliner across the upper eyelids. I liked the way it looked so much I continued to wear it like that even after the lashes grew back. No one was able to tell I did not have eyelashes. In fact, I was out one night talking to someone, and my eyes kept tearing. I just fanned my face and said, "It's really smoky in here." The person couldn't tell that I was lacking eyelashes, and the real reason for my tears was that the particles in the air wreaked havoc on my eyes.

Throughout all of my experiences, I continually found new and improved ways to have fun with my hair or apply my makeup. Eventually, I became daring and creative. Now I enjoy trying new approaches to hair or makeup, whether it is the cut, color, what makeup I buy, or how I apply it. I am open to change and have thus ascended from my cosmetic rut. My apprehension and fear of life's changes are gone forever!

Perk 4
Becoming an Organized Person

Throughout the entire experience, without even realizing it, I was finally getting organized. Before I got sick, I had never been an organized person. Becoming organized had always been my biggest goal—and it seemed impossible to achieve. I always used to lose one earring, whether it was from a pair I bought at the flea market or the Diamond Exchange. Or I would be running around the house in the morning looking for the shoes that I needed to wear, the ones that were the *only* pair that matched the suit I had on. I even had trouble keeping my room neat. At twenty-five years old, I think I should have been capable of keeping a neat room. (It was always clean, just a mess!)

But, ironically, one of the best things about my having cancer was how it helped me to become an extremely organized person.

In addition to everything else I had going on in my life at that time, all of a sudden I had to handle the insurance companies, state disability, Social Security disability, all of the medical procedures, and so much more. I had to handle much of it myself because neither my parents nor my sisters could have filled out the paperwork or answered the questions over the phone (such as an interview with Social Security disability). It was my responsibility.

However, because I spent most of the first six months in the hospital, my mother took care of my bills and all of the medical insurance issues, such as explanations of my benefits and phone calls from doctors looking for their payments. One time, I walked into the house and saw my mother sitting on the floor with a bunch of insurance benefits forms in a circle around her. When I asked what she was doing, she told me she was trying to organize them according to the date of service. Mom is organized!

My mother, father and sisters pulled together and did whatever they could to help me get through the initial shock. Being diagnosed with cancer was undoubtedly the ultimate of unexpected curves. My sense of control, as I once knew it, was gone. As the spiraling began, I became uneasy and confused. As it continued, I became fearful and anxious. I waited for my nightmare to end so that when I awoke I could resume my pre-diagnosis life. The only problem was that my nightmare was a reality. My whole world was shaken, as if an earthquake erupted within my being.

As this happened to me, I experienced the emotions. When I was told I had lymphoblastic lymphoma and that it was a rapidly growing mass, that was bad enough. But when the doctors explained that if the chemotherapy they were about to give me didn't work just as rapidly then I could be dead within a month, that was preposterous to me—an unthinkable reality.

I've already described my reaction to the news of a two and a half year protocol, but to hear that I was a goner if the chemo didn't work right away was way beyond comprehension. The confusion, sadness, terror, massive anxiety and anger surrounding the worst case scenario were too much for me to handle.

A few days before they started the chemotherapy, and after I heard all about the protocol and the "what if it doesn't work speech," a social worker from Sloan-Kettering entered my room. She referred to me as Margaret and asked how I was feeling. I was in an angry mood. I was so angry I wanted to kick the door down and walk out as if this was not happening. I responded, "Who are you? *And*, my name is Erin, E-R-I-N, *Erin*! My formal name is Margaret Erin Heenan; however, no one's ever called me Margaret a day in my life." I continued, "If you're going to come in and ask me how I'm feeling, knowing I was just diagnosed with cancer, at least get my name right."

She apologized.

"Get your records straight. I've told every doctor and every nurse that's spoken with me so far to please call me Erin. I do not go by Margaret. You are a social worker. I would have expected that you would check these things out before coming into this room."

As if I wasn't annoyed enough, she asked me why I didn't like the name Margaret.

Exhausted, I answered, "There is nothing wrong with the name Margaret. I was the first grandchild and my parents named me after my grandmother. But *no one* has ever called me anything but Erin—not my parents, or any of my family or friends."

She apologized and said someone should have made a note on the chart that I should be addressed as Erin. She promised it wouldn't happen again.

"I am so sorry!" I cried, experiencing a massive mood swing. "It's not your fault. I'm taking everything out on you right now because you were the one who walked in the room at the wrong time. I need help. I don't know how to handle this!" I cried hysterically, while yelling at the same time.

The social worker wanted me to try and stay focused on what was right with my life.

"There is nothing right with my life right now, nothing," I said coldly with my hands in the air and my eyebrows twisted.

She asked if the doctors had a protocol that could possibly cure me.

"Yeah."

Then she asked if I had family and friends who love me and are concerned.

"Yeah, but I'm going to be bald and throwing my guts up all day long," I said defensively (experiencing a mood swing yet again), as if I was implying she didn't know what she was talking about.

The social worker said she would come back if I wanted to talk to her about how I was feeling, or if I needed anything at all. She handed me her business card and walked out the door.

It was June. It looked beautiful outside, but I couldn't go out. I was trapped on a hospital bed about an hour from my house, sitting Indian style by myself in a pair of shorts and a tee-shirt.

"Hi, Erin. Could you help me?" I heard through the hospital curtain.

I thought I was by myself, but then I quickly realized there was another person in the room. "Uh, hold on." I said. "I'll open the curtain."

"I know you're a little upset right now, but I was wondering if you could do me a favor," my roommate said.

I saw this woman, about thirty years older than me, with all of these tubes attached to her. She wore a smile that was more of a compassionate smile than an "I'm so happy right now" kind of smile.

Calmly, I asked, "What do you need?"

"A cup of water please. And if you could read my Bible to me I would appreciate it." She continued, "I have breast cancer, stomach cancer, and liver cancer. I hope you could read the Good Book to me."

There have been very few times in my life when I've experienced an epiphany. My roommate became one of them. "Sure," I said with a smile. "Here's your cup of water. Whenever you need it refilled just tell me, okay? I see the bookmark in your Bible, would you like me to read from that page?" I asked.

"That would be nice, Erin," she said, looking as if she was truly grateful.

As I read, my newfound roommate did not realize she was the one who did me the favor. That woman had more cancer than I did, and no one to come and visit. We were roommates for approximately two weeks and I credit her for my second mental transformation. The first was when my sisters and I planned a party from my room—I had a future living with cancer. The second was my hospital roommate's acceptance of her situation with such grace and peace. I learned a great deal from her disposition.

Needless to say, with her permission, I kept the curtain open the whole time and my company became her company as well. Every night we were together, close to bedtime, I read the Bible, and made sure she was comfortable.

After that, I reached deep within the realm of who I was, regrouped, and pulled out the strength and will of a survivor. I began to establish some sort of control over my life once again. I kept telling myself it was me against the cancer, and I would win! As I experienced nausea from the chemotherapy, tiredness as a result of the painkillers and tranquilizers, fever as a reaction to low blood counts, and even depression arising from the whole experience, I never gave up the control I seemed to have over my own health and well-being. Although there were grave physiological and psychological tolls to be paid, I refused to throw my hands in the air as if to say, "Whatever happens, happens!" I felt that doing so would have been surrendering to the disease, and for me that was not an option.

Even though I found this well of strength deep within myself, I did choose to speak with a therapist after my protocol ended, and it turned out to be the greatest thing for me. I wish I had gone while I was in treatment—chemotherapy, radiation, procedures, and everything else it took to cure me of non-Hodgkins lymphoblastic lymphoma. But it was only when it was all over, when the protocol ended, that I crashed. I fought the disease for so long, never throwing my hands in the air as if to give up—not for a moment—but eventually it caught up to me. My therapist said that the depression and anxiety I was feeling was called post-traumatic stress syndrome, similar to what a soldier experiences after coming home from war. She helped me put as much as we could into perspective—she called it "compartmentalizing." Therapy did, and, whenever the need arises, still does, help me immensely.

Another extremely important thing I did was stay on top of my protocol. The doctors did not want to overwhelm me in the beginning, so they gave me, I believe, one month's schedule at a time. Therefore, I knew exactly what medications were due and when the followup tests should be performed. I always checked my schedule before heading out to the hospital.

Doctors are human and sometimes make mistakes. It was very important for me to make sure I knew what was going on. There were a few occasions when the doctor thought I was due for one chemotherapy treatment (say, the Cytoxan chemo agent), when, in fact, I was due for a different one (say, Adriamycin). I'd let my doctor know, and the adjustment would be made.

Taking prescribed medicine may sound easy, but it isn't if you're taking about thirty pills a day like I was. I was determined not to be one of those people who occasionally forgot to take a pill and then took double the dose—I knew I'd be asking for problems.

My father helped me stay on top of things by helping me write up a medicine schedule. I drew columns on a piece of loose-leaf paper. Each medication had its own column. On the left-hand side, going from the top of the page to the bottom I wrote the dates for that month. Across the top of the page in each column, I listed the names of the medications I was taking. Then, within each box, I wrote the time I took the medication. It was because of this system that I never forgot whether I had taken a medication.

For instance, if I had to take Methotrexate four times a day, in the Methotrexate column I wrote the specific times I took the medication next to the date of that day. So if I was supposed to take four on that day, I knew there should have been four different times noted in its box by the end of the day. Similarly, if I needed Percocet three times a day, there should have been three different times in the box for that day in the Percocet column. That system worked for me because I maintained control over my never-ending supply of medications.

After a while, establishing and maintaining control of my medical situation became second nature. Another example of this had to do with inconvenient medical appointments. In the beginning, I found the appointments that I was given were inconvenient. I was not a morning person, and I hated sitting in traffic. I had to travel for approximately forty-five minutes (without traffic) into Manhattan from Garden City, Long Island, a few times per week, and my appointments were usually before ten o'clock. Initially, being the kind of person I was, I just did as I was told and never complained. I knew I did not want to handle the cancer half-cocked by choosing a hospital closer to home—inconvenience was never a factor when it came to making me healthy again. However, since both of my parents worked, my Aunt Rita, Uncle Brian, and eventually my boyfriend (now husband) Ronnie were usually the ones who took turns taking me into the city for my treatments, and they were great about it.

Aunt Rita and I usually took the same route, traffic or not, into the city and went directly to the parking lot. After the treatments, she and

I scouted out all of the restaurants in the vicinity. Aunt Rita generously took me out to eat after treatments, when I was up to it. It always gave me something to look forward to when I was through at the hospital.

Uncle Brian was very funny. He worked for the New York City fire department at the time and knew a thousand shortcuts into Manhattan to avoid traffic. Once we arrived in the city, we would begin to scope out a regular parking space on the street to avoid having to pay for garage parking. He usually knew of a secret few. It was like our private little challenge, and when someone else beat us to it, we felt defeated. It was rare, but when it happened, we just held our heads high and looked to park in a nearby parking lot. It's funny how something like that became an adventure. Every time I went for chemotherapy with Uncle Brian, I looked forward to the many laughs we would have.

Ronnie's approach was very similar to Uncle Brian's. He used to work in Manhattan and, at that time, drove into the city every day, so he knew a thousand ways to get there as well. I'm much more like Aunt Rita. Put me on the road that I know, and traffic or not, that's the way I go every time. With Ronnie, I'd end up on all of these different parkways having no idea where I was. Sometimes we took the tunnel and drove uptown, sometimes we took the bridges. He knew when to listen to the radio to get the traffic information so we could avoid the bumper to bumper. It was too funny. After visits to the oncologist, Ronnie and I would either go back to his apartment to hang out, or we would go and do something fun.

As time went by, the four of us concluded that when we went for the treatments, whether it was Aunt Rita and I, Uncle Brian and I, or Ronnie and I, it was usually better in the late afternoon. The wait in the waiting room was much shorter, and afterwards we went out for dinner in the city or on the way home. By doing that, for the most part, we were able to avoid rush hour traffic. It was great! My aunt, uncle, and Ronnie made my ordeal so much easier to deal with. They helped me maintain my sense of humor, which, in my opinion, became part of the cure. Laughter really is the best medicine.

I had a choice: I could spend the length of my treatment period going to appointments at times that were dictated to me by the doctor's receptionist, or I could make appointments that were convenient for me. It took months for me to realize that I could do the latter. As I said, I was not a morning person; therefore, I stopped settling for morning appointments. I could have gone the entire two and a half years being managed by my medical ordeal, but instead I incorporated it into my life and I managed *it*.

By staying on top of my protocol, I felt that I established and maintained as much control as I could have. It helped me reduce the number of surprises that were to come my way, but that is not to say there were not many more surprises in store for me.

I tell this story to cancer patients I meet just so they won't make the same mistake I did. Toward the end of the protocol, my liver functions were somewhat abnormal, so before receiving chemotherapy they had to be tested. If the blood test came back within a certain range, then it was all right to follow through with the treatment. However, if the numbers were high, then the treatment had to be postponed.

One day I went for chemotherapy and the doctor seemed to be in a rush. He was not my main oncologist, but another doctor filling the chemotherapy prescription. He was well aware of my medical history, and in the past had given me similar liver function tests and chemotherapy treatments. On this particular day, however, he was in such a hurry that he spilled Betadine all over the exam room and seemed to have rushed the treatment. That specific treatment, called intrathecal methotrexate, involved injecting chemotherapy directly into the brain—obviously, a procedure not to be rushed. Despite that, the doctor failed to check my liver functions. It was at that point that I should have stopped everything and demanded the blood test be done. But instead, I assumed he was acting professionally and knew what he was doing. I went on blind faith, something that will never happen again. The treatment was performed and, as usual for that stage of my protocol (the maintenance phase), I was scheduled to start medications that were to be taken at home in pill form, orally, for one month. Those medications were called Methotrexate and 6-MP. These chemotherapy drugs directly affect the liver. After the "rushed" intrathecal methotrexate treatment was over, I went home and became sick for hours. Hours turned into days. As I started taking the chemotherapy pills, I became even more debilitated and was constantly getting sick. It became so bad that I did not have the strength to walk from the bedroom to the bathroom, and the whites of my eyes were turning yellow. I felt as if I was dying. I called my main oncologist and he told me to stop all medications. He tested my liver functions and, as I suspected, they were through the roof. They were so high that I ended up with drug-induced hepatitis.

When I went back to ream out the doctor who treated me for his incompetence, I asked him why he did not check my liver functions before putting me on heavy duty medications that directly affect the liver. As the vein in his forehead bulged, his response to me was that I looked fine that day. Yeah, with a wig and some makeup I always looked fine! What kind of a doctor would not check the liver *before* treatment, knowing the patient's liver functions have been abnormal for close to a year? The doctor could not even look me in the eye as we spoke. I gave him some choice words and left. It was a bittersweet moment for me—bitter because I was so sick, and sweet because I never had to have chemotherapy ever again. As I stated earlier, the maintenance phase of the protocol was to be repeated every three months for two years. But because of the drug-induced hepatitis, I did not have to go through the last three-month sequence. My oncologist said it did not make a difference because I had two and a half years of treatment under my belt. It was finally over!

After that treacherous experience, I swore to myself that I will always second-guess the doctors whenever I feel it is necessary. I would not worry about insulting them or making them feel as if they are incapable of doing their jobs. A good doctor appreciates a patient who is aware of what is happening and thinks for him/herself, without worrying about possible bruises to the doctor's ego.

There were many important lessons learned from my hepatitis experience. In every aspect of my life, followup became extremely important. I no longer left anything to chance, whether it was medically related or otherwise. I have become a lot more thorough in everything I do. One example of this is that if I'm due for a CT scan, MRI, endoscopy, or anything else that needs scheduling, I do not wait for the doctor's office to call me. I have it on my calendar— many times they don't call. I also realized that the expression "no news is good news" is a farce. If I needed results from whatever medical test I'd had, I learned that I should call the doctor after a reasonable amount of time had passed. Sometimes my results were misplaced or never received by the doctor. Therefore, a phone call from me was necessary.

Another example is that when I send something to someone, no matter who it is, I call or e-mail to make sure it arrived safely and on time. I keep files of important documentation, and make sure my family's information is in order. This has definitely helped me maintain order in my life.

I went from being totally unorganized to—I am proud to say— being exceedingly organized! My experience definitely helped me establish and maintain control over the factors in my life that needed to be organized. Once that happened, everything else fell into place and I established order in my life beyond my wildest dreams. What a perk!

Perk 5
Discovering I'm Even Stronger than Before!

Another one of the many perks is that experiencing this life-threatening and life-altering condition brought me to a physical, emotional, and psychological comfort level with who I am.

Throughout my life, I had always given credence to what other people thought about me, more so even than what I thought about myself. It was as if my family, teachers, bosses, and just about anyone had an opinion about who I was and the kind of person I was. These opinions seemed more credible to me than my own self-assessment. My true self-identity became more and more obscured as I gave increasing validation to everyone else's projected image of who I was.

However, when I was conforming to meet the needs of society in a way that went against my moral, ethical, and general personal standards, then I was conforming at a serious personal price. I found myself at times capitulating who I was little by little, to the point where it seemed I was running away from myself. I felt as though I had become spiritually and emotionally separated from who I was fundamentally. My very essence became clouded by outside influences, and I began to lose my sense of self.

Pre-diagnosis, I was living life, more or less, like a spectator, going day to day, watching my life as an outsider. I would never think to ask, *Who am I?* But when I was lying in the hospital bed, near death, this question barraged my mind. After years of adapting to the social needs and expectations of my parents, teachers, bosses, and so on, I came to a screeching halt. I wanted to know what made Erin Heenan...Erin Heenan. This was when my passionate soul-searching began. It was as if I hardly knew myself. I experienced this incredible urge to go deeper within to find my true essence, the reason for my existence.

I meditated from the hospital bed and at home. The meditation tapes I purchased were priceless. Lying down in the bed, the tape would go as follows: "Feel the heels of your feet on the bed; they are part of you. Relax your heels and let them sink deeper and deeper into the bed. Feel your feet ... feel your toes ..." The tape would go on for forty-five minutes covering my entire body, allowing me to *connect* with my body, to take the moment to feel each and every part of it, and to relax my body at the same time. The tapes also dealt with breathing techniques. As the meditation went on, I was told to breathe the positive energy in and release the negative energy with the outward breath.

There were other meditation tapes that helped me visualize my inner self—more of a "mind over matter" visualization meditation. I learned that my body was not just skin covering a meaningless inside. The view I had of myself was being clarified with every thought, every breath, and every heartbeat. Eventually, I knew my body inside and out. In addition, I began tapping into my inner strength, which led me down the path toward a stronger mental and intellectual discipline.

An example of this was a couple of months into my protocol (by which time I had a lot of meditation under my belt), when I had to stay in the hospital for five days of round-the-clock chemotherapy. The nurses gave me some sort of pre-medication that had me slipping in and out of consciousness. My father stayed with me the whole time until I fell asleep. When the nurses suggested that he leave because I was going to be out for hours, he complied with great reluctance. I continued drifting in and out of consciousness.

After what I believe was an hour or so, I saw my younger cousin, Kristoffer, sitting in the chair next to my bed. I would describe Krissy as being rough and tough around the edges, but with a heart of gold on the inside. At first I thought I was hallucinating. I was hardly able to speak. After mustering up all the strength I could, I asked him to leave so I would not cause him undo stress and anxiety. Kristoffer refused and insisted he was not leaving my side. At that moment, I saw traits in my nineteen-year-old cousin that I never expected. I always knew Kristoffer was caring, but I never realized the depth of his compassion until then. At that moment, I saw that Krissy was no longer a kid—he was a man. To this day, I tell him that no matter what happens, I will never forget that he was there for me when I *really* needed him.

After the week of round-the-clock chemotherapy ended, my father picked me up and took me home. He and my mother tried to keep me as comfortable as possible. My father brought in my favorite cookies, but I just could not eat them. I saw the tears well up in his eyes, so I did my best to eat one or two. Normally I would have been able to eat ten or twenty, so you can imagine my father's disappointment.

When I was nauseous, the thought of food, no matter how delicious, brought about the possibility of throwing up. Throwing up was something I was never good at. I detested it! There were many times when I probably should have thrown up, but I refused to allow it. I stayed nauseous instead. This is where mind over matter plays a role. I can count on one hand the number of times that I threw up from that rigorous protocol of two and half years of combination chemotherapy.

I truly believe it's mind over matter. However, I sometimes think that all of those years prior to being diagnosed, when stopping off at the diner with my friends on the way home on a Friday or Saturday night for an "early breakfast" was routine, or—my all-time favorite—having 7-11 nachos with chili and cheese at all hours of the night/morning (or whenever, for that matter), might have been the prep work for the iron stomach I needed to tolerate the chemotherapy.

After being discharged, I was only home for a few days. The round-the-clock chemotherapy had knocked my blood count down to zero. I developed a fever, which meant I had to go back into the hospital immediately and be put on antibiotics. The only thing I had to look forward to was Aunt Rita's daily supply of ice cream shakes and UB's (Uncle Brian's) awesome cooking.

The doctors tried different medications, which were unsuccessful. They could not figure out where the infection was coming from. The only alternative was an antibiotic called amphotericin, also known as "shake and bake" because your body gets an intense case of the chills, which is so uncontrollable that your back hurts from shaking. Following an episode of that, you sweat to the point of soaking your clothes—hence the term "shake and bake." Those treatments were given every night for six hours and lasted close to a week.

I was normally the kind of patient who was easygoing, positive, and upbeat. However, after a few nights of shake and bake, I felt as though I was a rag doll. Happy and upbeat were becoming a mere memory. I could not walk to the bathroom, and the nurses had to change my sweaty clothes. I begged the doctor to end the treatments. I literally was on the floor with my arms around his legs begging him to let them end. The doctor responded that it was a matter of life or death, and he had to continue the treatments in order to make me well.

My mother and a very close friend of the family, Lydia, came to visit. They did not realize they were walking into a horror show. I was in the middle of a treatment and trembling irrepressibly. My mother and Lydia had to leave. No one should have to encounter seeing their daughter in such a state.

That night, one of the nurses came into my room to check on me, and I asked if I was going to be all right. He started crying and told me it did not look good, that I should prepare for the worst. I became so petrified I could not close my eyes for fear I would never see morning. I just looked at him and said, "No, I'm sorry, but you're wrong. I will not have you sitting here believing that I'm going to die. I'd like for you to think positive thoughts for me. Maybe your positive energy along with mine will help me through this. Please don't tell me or even allude to the fact that I'm going to die!"

The nurse agreed with me and apologized as he wiped his tears on the way out the door.

I meditated, visualizing the good cells destroying the bad cells, relaxing my body so I could focus, seriously focus, tapping into the mental state of thinking and feeling that everything would be okay— the white light that I saw throughout my body would clean out any harmful clouds within me as I consciously inhaled healthy energy and exhaled the negative.

Morning came, and with that a telephone call from my Aunt Nancy to see how I was doing. I was exhausted mentally and physically from being up all night, the chemo, and everything else that was going on. I started crying. And, in a weak moment, I asked Aunt Nancy if I was going to die. She started crying and stayed on the phone with me for quite a while. I cannot remember exactly what she said; nevertheless, her words were comforting and gave me the strength to get back on track. I refused to let the disease get the best of me. It was me against the cancer, and I was claiming victory.

The end result was exactly that! The fever dissipated, and my blood counts were out of the danger range. I was finally free to go home after being in the hospital for close to a month. What a great feeling!

A few weeks later I went back to the hospital again for a scheduled routine appointment. After walking through the doors to the exam room with Uncle Brian, my oncologist told me I had to go back soon for another five-day treatment of round-the-clock chemo. I still hadn't recuperated from the first experience mentally and physically, and I was petrified to go through it again so soon. But the doctor said I had no choice—I had to stay on protocol. I was visibly upset and shaken.

When we left the hospital, Uncle Brian said, "Why don't we go look at the tree in Rockefeller Plaza." It was a cold, dark November's night. All I remember was standing next to my uncle, looking at the tree, and thinking that I should try my best to enjoy this experience of being in Manhattan looking at the renowned Christmas tree because I didn't know what was going to happen when I started the treatments again. On the way home, Uncle Brian took me to a restaurant called Donovan's, where they have great burgers. He tried so hard to make the night a nice one for me—and it worked. It was a delightful distraction from what was to come, and I had an enjoyable night out with my uncle.

As I've said in the past, I took control of my medical treatments and medications, stayed on top of my protocol, and scheduled more convenient appointments (over time I've learned that a long wait in any doctor's office is more the norm than not). In addition to that, I always followed the doctor's orders with total compliance. He was the professional at curing the cancer I had, not me. I just learned how to have the experience move forward more smoothly. However, there were times I was left with no alternative but to stand my ground.

An example of one of those times was approximately five months into the protocol when I went into the hospital for that second round of the five-day round-the-clock chemo treatment. It was the same kind as I described before, only this time I flatly refused to develop a fever. Before I was admitted, I just told my body, *No—I will not get a fever.* Every time a doctor or nurse mentioned that a fever was more probable than possible because I would not have any blood counts to fight off infection, I refused to listen. I knew I had ended up with the fever the last time and that I had needed the treacherous "shake and bake," along with six blood transfusions and many other medications to keep me alive. It was for those reasons that I tried my best to prevent myself from being in that predicament again. I repeated over and over in my head—*I will NOT get a fever. My body temperature will stay as is, thankyouverymuch!* It was the only fever I'd had thus far and I was not going through that hellish nightmare again.

After being admitted to the hospital for that second round, not wanting to be there and thoroughly exhausted, I continued to meditate and visualize. *When I'm discharged, I will live my life as normally as possible without getting a fever.*

As I was reading one of my self-help books, a doctor, whom I had never met before, came into my room declaring her intention to implement the intrathecal methotrexate treatment (the one in which the Ommaya shunt in my brain was accessed). The first step was the extraction of cerebral spinal fluid, which would be tested, followed by the injection of chemotherapy. The whole procedure takes about fifteen minutes.

Normally, the doctor had me lie down on the hospital bed and tilted the bed so my head was lower than my feet. This new doctor, however, gave me the treatment as I sat straight up on the bed. I explained how my main oncologist performed the procedure, and she told me not to be concerned with what she was doing. Halfway through her treatment, I felt something dripping down the side of my head, a sensation I had never felt in the past. I interrupted the procedure, ran to the bathroom, and threw up. The doctor said she would try again later and left. After a while, she returned and tried repeatedly with little success. I threw up again and again. This went on all day. It reached the point where, whenever I saw that doctor come through the door to my room, I ran to the bathroom and threw up.

Finally, I overheard her speaking with another doctor saying something to the effect that she had never given this kind of treatment before and she was nervous. Well, I confronted her inexperience, letting her know I overheard what she was discussing, and told her she was never to come near me again. I quickly learned that if you have knowledge that a doctor has never performed a specific procedure, you can refuse his or her services and demand someone with experience. From that point on, prior to *any* procedure, I asked every doctor who I did not recognize how experienced he or she was to prevent that from happening again.

After the week of round-the-clock chemotherapy was over, my father picked me up once again. When I walked through the door to our house, I told my parents that I wasn't going to get a fever this time. I told them that I didn't care what the doctors, nurses, or anyone else said; it's not happening. I continued to live my life, going out with my friends, golfing, taking long walks, and anything and everything that I would have done on a day off when I was pre-cancer, only now, on a much deeper level, not taking *anything* for granted and using common sense. I made sure not to expose myself to adults who were obviously sick, or little children who went to school. I was told by a nurse that those things would guarantee me a bed back at Sloan-Kettering.

When I went to my oncologist's office for a followup visit, everyone was amazed that I had not ended up back in the hospital. It was extremely rare for someone to escape infection, even if they never left their house. I, on the other hand, enjoyed my time out of the hospital. I believe it was the result of my tenacious determination, inner resources, and powerful mind. Mind over matter is more than a cliché, it's a life saver!

After everything I had gone through during the first six months of my protocol, and as time went on, I finally reached a clearing where what people thought of me, no matter who they were, became secondary, or even meaningless when compared to my self-assessment. The whole experience was quite liberating, and at last I feel whole and at peace with who I am. I no longer look to anyone for approval for anything. I just look deep within my own heart and soul and trust my own judgment.

Pre-diagnosis, when I was drifting through life, I had always been one to root for and help the underdog. Asserting myself for the benefit of others was never a problem, but asserting myself for my own benefit was next to impossible. Post-diagnosis, that became a completely different story. The decisions to be made at that point were a matter of life or death—my own! I began asserting myself left, right, and sideways. I became my own most aggressive advocate. I tenaciously defended and protected myself—yet another perk, exemplifying how good comes out of bad.

My ability to make demands was another indication of how I became less passive and more assertive—stronger, not weaker, post-diagnosis. As a patient, I was in the position to demand what was rightfully due me. I had the right to demand professional, courteous, non-intimidating, experienced, timely, informative, and ethical services. *Making demands and asserting myself became part of my survival.*

On the other hand, there were times when I asked the doctor how experienced he was with regard to a particular part of my protocol, whether it was chemo or radiation treatments, procedures such as bone marrow biopsies or spinal taps, or even surgeries, and the doctor reassured me that he had done whatever was about to be done many times in the past without a problem… except for the following incident.

As I've stated previously in this book, I want to share mistakes I made so that others can learn from them. I hope that if others can learn from my experiences, instances such as the following can be avoided by anyone in a situation similar to mine.

Three months into chemotherapy, I had a metaport implanted in my chest with a tube going up to the vein in my neck. The metaport was imperative, since the veins in my arms had collapsed due to the toxic medications being injected.

During the consultation prior to the surgery, I said to the doctor, "I know we don't have any other choice; it's just that I can't believe that not only am I bald and everything else, but now I'm going to have a huge lump sticking out of my chest as well."

The doctor understood my concern and suggested that he put the metaport deeper into my chest so the lump from the metaport wouldn't be as obvious. I agreed. At the time I didn't realize that when it was deeper and less noticeable, it was more painful to access because the needle had to go through more skin tissue to get to the metaport. The doctors or nurses who tried to access the metaport would ask me to put my shoulders back as far as I could with my chest stretching forward. That brought the metaport as close to the surface of the skin as possible; however, it was still buried pretty deep. My mentality during those times, though, was that when I looked good, I felt good. So the pain took a back seat.

Through the accessed metaport, the chemotherapy was injected and blood was extracted for testing. It alleviated many of the unpleasant side effects the veins endured, such as burning and possible leakage. Aside from the discomfort, the metaport was a great instrument. My treatments ended a little over two years after the metaport was installed. However, my doctor felt it was best to keep it in for an extra year. The rationale behind his decision was based on the possibility of reoccurrence of the disease.

Finally, three years from when the metaport was put in, the day came for it to be removed. The foreign instrument was going to be gone forever! I was so excited to finally get rid of the metaport that I actually looked forward to the surgery. There was going to be one less reminder of the disease and one less medical inconvenience to follow up on. Ronnie drove me into the city for the surgery. The two of us discussed how great I would feel afterwards. We were both very enthusiastic about the pending procedure. The chemotherapy had been over for a year and now this was the final chapter of the last three and a half years of my life dealing with cancer and everything that came with it. The only problem was that we had no idea what I was in for once I arrived at the hospital.

Following protocol, I checked in at the front desk and sat down until they called my name. Once called, I was escorted to the dressing room to change into a hospital gown. I was feeling elated that it was almost over. A few minutes later, I was taken into the room where the surgery was to be performed. I met the doctor and the nurse. As I lay down on the operating table, the doctor said he was going to numb the area of my chest where the metaport was located. I found it strange that they were not going to administer anesthesia so I questioned the doctor. He reassured me that these types of metaports simply fall out, and since there was not going to be a lot of cutting or maneuvering, anesthesia was unnecessary. Without knowing any better, I trusted that the doctor knew what he was doing, and we proceeded. After injecting some lidocaine, a numbing agent, the doctor began the surgery. Once he was in my chest, he realized there was a tremendous amount of scar tissue surrounding both the metaport and the tube that went up to the vein in my neck.

He began to sweat and stated his concern. The doctor said he was under the impression the metaport was in my chest for six months. At six months or less, they usually fall out. Mine was in for approximately three years. Consequently, scar tissue had grown around the metaport, adhering it to my body.

As the doctor, with great trepidation, continued the surgery, he explained to the nurse that I was in the wrong part of the hospital and that I should have had some kind of anesthesia. When I requested to be transported to the appropriate part of the hospital, the doctor declined and told me everything would be okay—he was capable of removing it without a problem. Innocently (or should I say naively), I agreed to stay put out of trust. In hindsight, I should have insisted they put me on a gurney and bring me to the part of the hospital where I belonged.

The surgery continued, and to my astonishment, there was not as much as a painkiller available. The doctor and the nurse continued to run into problems, as they needed to resort to electric knives and all sorts of instruments to try to cut out the metaport that had been engulfed by my body. I had to deny my urge to jump up off the table and run as fast as my legs would carry me. I could not stop crying. I just lay still and said repeatedly, "This is disgusting, this is disgusting, please stop, it's disgusting." Finally, I could not take the pain any longer, so, through my tears, I began screaming uncontrollably, "Stop, please stop!" My screams were so loud that Ronnie heard them all the way down the long corridor and around the corner in the waiting room. He panicked and tried to get to me, but the administrator would not allow it. Screaming was not typical of my reactions. On the contrary, I was always the type of patient to "grin and bear it." This was not turning out to be the kind of day we had been anticipating.

Upon completion of the surgery, the doctor ordered a prescription of Percocet painkillers to be filled promptly by the hospital's pharmacy. I considered it to be too little too late. I kept thinking, *Please, someone, just hit me over the head with a brick and knock me out, so when I wake up the Percocet will have kicked in!*

My chest experienced such physical trauma that there was swelling the size of a golf ball in the area where the metaport once was. The swelling took months to dissipate and, to this day, many years later, I still do not have the range of motion I once had with my right arm prior to the whole metaport experience.

But then again, to exemplify good coming out of bad, I attribute my improved golf game to my slightly impaired range of motion. Ronnie will attest to how it seems to have improved my golf swing. Bizarre, but true.

Throughout my life, since childhood, I've gained more and more confidence and strength when dealing with issues as they come. Whether it be taking on the school bully, telling my married boss that he was out of line for coming on to me, or informing doctors when mistakes were being made with regard to my care, each negative experience was a learning one and made me stronger. It's been a continuous process for me that I'm sure will continue all throughout my life.

Perk 6
Falling in Love While Going for Chemotherapy

When I was bombarded with the bad news of the diagnosis, I felt that marriage might never be a part of my future. If I had already been in a relationship or married, I might have felt that our connection was to be tested, with who knows what consequences.

Initially, I thought I had to put my love life on the back burner. I was certain it would be impossible for me to have a serious relationship for three years, and then I hoped someone would accept me with all of my medical "faults." I found myself going out on one or two dates with someone, then ending it out of fear they would find out I was stigmatized with disease. I never expected that within nine months post-diagnosis, love would bloom and change my life completely.

As I've said, I was single when I received the heart-wrenching news. Depressing thoughts started to invade my mind. I thought, *I'll never marry. Who would want someone plagued with disease— a damaged package?* The wild, unruly, indomitable visions ravaged through my mind's eye. Having never met a young person with cancer before, all I could picture was that I would look similar to the zombies I saw in horror flicks. My bald head, hairless body, gray complexion, scars from surgeries, bruises from needles, constant smell of vomit, and screams of fright or pain in the middle of the night—they were all I imagined every idle moment I had.

As time went on, I began to have a better understanding of what I looked like bald and gray, with bruises, scars, and everything else. My initial mental picture was nowhere near reality—the zombie I thought I'd see in the mirror was nonexistent. The visions were only imagined and brought about by vulnerability.

Vulnerability in itself is the condition of being exposed to something detrimental. That said, I understand how easily these emotions affected me. Cancer patients become extremely vulnerable when thrown into a world of detriment. Once diagnosed, I felt as though I was vincible, and that the disease could overcome me at any moment. As time went on, though, after a lot of mental processing and paying attention to what needed to be done to make me well again, I recognized that my safeguard, shelter, and shield was my protocol in conjunction with my optimistic outlook. If I had wallowed in the vulnerable state, it would have done nothing but *undermine* who I was in terms of courage, boldness, and bravery.

After spending much time working this out emotionally, psychologically, and physically, praying to God, and slowly accepting that I looked fine with a wig and makeup, I did not allow my fortitude to be undermined.

I started to have a better understanding of what I was dealing with, and part of me began to think that maybe there was still a chance that someone would accept me for who I was, regardless of my temporary medical status.

In the beginning of my protocol, when a guy asked me out, I'd always thanked him for the offer, but then made up some reason why

I couldn't go. However, one night, about eight months into my protocol, I was up in Hunter Mountain, New York, with friends. I met a very nice guy who asked me out to dinner, and *with great trepidation* I said yes. He lived close to me, so we set up the date when I'd meet him at the bar/restaurant we decided on. I didn't know him well enough to have him pick me up from my house. I didn't like dates knowing where I lived if I didn't already know them to begin with. I would always think, *What if he turns out to be a nut? Now he knows where I live.*

So, I was out on a date with a very nice guy, someone I definitely would have gone out with again. Then, halfway through the night, my cousin Barbara came into the bar/restaurant and introduced me to her friends, one of whom was Ronnie. I spent a few minutes talking to him, and he left me with such an incredible impression. I asked my date if he would mind if I stayed to talk with my cousin. He agreed. When the date ended, he went home and I spent the rest of the night talking to Ronnie. It was as if we had an immediate connection.

I saw him the following week at the same place. He came over to me, touched my hair, and told me I looked great. *Oh man*, I thought, whining, *Do anything—spill a drink on me by accident, trip over me, anything.* The touching of my wig was an instant buzz-kill for me, more so even than if I had fallen on my face. I thanked him for the compliment, ran to my sister, Katie and asked her if she would mind explaining my situation to Ronnie. I was having too much fun. To have engaged in a conversation about cancer when everyone is out trying to have a good time was meaningless to me, especially if it didn't go over well. I didn't want it to ruin my night, but I also didn't want to ruin anyone else's. So when I asked Katie to address it, I explained that if she was uncomfortable doing it, then I'd tell him myself and if he ran for cover, then so be it. Katie said she did not have a problem telling him.

Once Katie told Ronnie, his reaction was not only surprising, but encouraging as well. He told my sister that he admired my strength and courage and felt it made me a special person. Years later, Ronnie told me that he pointed me out to his friend Rob that night and said, "I'm going to marry that girl one day." He said that knowing I had cancer. After that night, we became inseparable.

Since my ordeal, the direction that my life has taken has been based on my own decisions, reactions, and perceptions, with how I perceive myself being most important. One day I might perceive a situation one way by seeing it through tired eyes, but the next day I might perceive the same situation in a completely different way after a good night's sleep. My perceptions were always changing, depending on my moods and how tired or sick I felt.

Initially, I was doing myself a great injustice by focusing on what was wrong with me. Only I was able to change my perception. I began saying positive things about myself out loud, so I was able to hear the words. I looked in the mirror and saw that gorgeous person inside and out, smiling back. I touched my heart and felt it beating. That represented life—my life! I concentrated on the positive and realized that my heightened awareness was beginning to see beauty and peace. I had nothing to stop me from falling in love but myself. Cancer and chemotherapy did not have to deter me from experiencing the world as a whole, and that included love.

I had just turned twenty-six and was nine months into my protocol when my relationship with Ronnie started out as friendship. We went golfing, to the movies, the bars, to lunch or dinner, and so on. We did everything together. Eventually, we became the best of friends. Ronnie wanted it to be more than that, but I did not want to start something because there were so many things wrong with me. I still had my love life on hold mentally and physically. I truly believed I couldn't handle a relationship at that stage of my life. So, I made up excuses for myself. For instance, he is three years younger than me, so I'd tell myself, *I can't go out with him, he's my cousin*

Barbara's age. Or, in my mind I felt as if my body had to be perfect in order to enter into a relationship. I never thought for a second that a gentleman would accept me as his girlfriend, hairless and with a blotchy gray complexion.

Six months went by and Ronnie's persistence never ended. "Erin, I really want to be more than just friends, but I don't want to jeopardize the friendship if you don't feel the same way," he said.

"Ronnie, look at me. I'm wearing a wig because I'm bald, for crying out loud. You're taking me to my treatments, surgeries, and everything else under the sun, and I don't want you to have to constantly worry about me." I continued, "You are a great friend! I'm just really uncomfortable with getting into a serious relationship while I'm in this condition," I said, wanting to cry but holding back.

"You see yourself so much worse than how I or anyone else that knows you sees you," he said.

I said, "Well, it's kind of like when someone has a zit on their face. That person feels as if it looks like Mount Rushmore. But, to everyone else it's not as noticeable. I get what you're saying, but I feel like I'm one big walking Mount Rushmore. So, can we just go have lunch and relax?" I asked.

I had someone who was so incredibly kind, considerate, handsome, intelligent, sensitive and, most importantly, sooo good to me. He loved me so much and I knew I loved him, but my medical situation kept me isolated—right up until that point! I decided I was going to overcome my fear and give love a chance. It was one of the hardest experiences of my life. I was extremely apprehensive, lacked confidence in this area at the time, and was filled with fear and anxiety. I was petrified of being rejected based on my physical condition after building up such a great friendship. If we entered into a serious relationship and then he second-guessed his decision, I don't know how I would have handled it.

As we sat at the table, me eating the lasagna and Ronnie eating the chicken parmesan, I kept thinking about the conversation we had in the car minutes before. *What is wrong with me?* I kept asking myself over and over as we ate. *Why is this harder than the chemo and everything else I've gone through? I want to be with him, but I'm not going to allow myself! What's up with that? What is wrong with me? This has to stop!*

After we had lunch, while driving home, I went out on that proverbial limb and conveyed my heartfelt feelings. At first I said, "You are so right. I'm being ridiculous. Can we start out just seeing each other at first?"

"No," Ronnie said. "I don't want to just see you. I want us to be committed to each other; not go around hanging out and seeing other people. I'm not into that." He continued, "I can see myself falling in love with you."

"Okay, okay. I'm just a *llliittlle* nervous, so I thought we'd start off slow. But you are too great a guy for me not to trust that things will work out." I joked, "So, are we officially boyfriend and girlfriend as of right now?"

"We are if you say we are. It's August tenth, so that'll be our official day that we started going out. Sound good?" he asked.

"Sounds great!" I said smiling.

Ronnie embraced my feelings wholeheartedly! He is unlike any guy I have ever met. Ronnie is strong, secure, sensitive, noble, and so even-keeled. He gave me the confidence to be secure with our relationship as it progressed further and further, finally culminating in true love.

One of my favorite quotes is from Henry Ford. It goes like this: "Whether you think you can or whether you think you can't, you're right." (Another one of my favorite quotes is from Helen Keller— "It's not why me, it's try me"—but that's for the next perk). For me, Ford's quote was incredibly inspiring. I kept telling myself that I *couldn't* enter into a relationship, so I didn't. As I reframed my way of thinking and began to believe that I *could* enter into a relationship, I did. There was no one keeping me from experiencing it but me. How liberating!

Over the years, Walt Disney World became our safe haven. When life became too much to handle, Ronnie and I went to the happiest place on earth. It was the mental break we needed from time to time. It released pent up nervous energy and stress. Everyone there is unbelievably nice, and everything is incredibly clean. We had nothing to worry about except taking in the scenery and enjoying ourselves. There was so much to do that it kept our minds off our problems. During the cancer ordeal, Ronnie and I must have gone to Disney in Florida at least five times. I was on all sorts of medications, including painkillers, tranquilizers, and anti-nausea pills. So there were plenty of times when I could not do a lot of walking. That was all right. We took our time, and Ronnie drove me back to the hotel to rest whenever I needed to. For us, it became our escape. Both of us had always loved Disney even long before we met, and it became the escape that we needed during some of the more trying times.

After one of my liver biopsies, we went once again to Disney. A liver biopsy is a procedure in which the doctors cannot administer any kind of anesthesia. I walked into the room, lay down on the table, looked at the doctor, then looked at the needle, which looked as if it was the length of my arm (no exaggeration). I took a deep breath in order to open up the ribcage and separate the lungs, which prevented my lung from being punctured. In my experience, when the needle went in, grabbed a piece of my liver, and came out again, it felt as if I had just been stabbed in the abdomen. I was not allowed to move, so when the needle went in, it was shocking how much it hurt. I wanted to jump fifty feet in the air, but couldn't. No anesthesia before and no painkillers after! What were the doctors thinking? (Someone has to rethink that process!) I don't know whether things have changed since I had my last liver biopsy, but if they haven't I suggest a mild tranquilizer before and some painkillers afterwards, just for peace of mind and quality of life.

When the procedure was over, I was taken up to a room in the hospital where they laid me down on my side and told me I had to stay that way for five hours. I could not even see who was coming in and out of my room because they faced me toward the window. At that time, I thought to myself, *Disney, definitely Disney!* Ronnie and I went one week later for three nights and four days. That was my silver lining.

Ronnie continued to take me to all of my chemotherapy treatments, doctors' visits, surgeries, procedures, radiology appointments, and so on. You name it, he took me! He became my rock and never once faltered. There were times after surgeries, treatments, or whatever I had done that day when Ronnie took me home, laid me down on the couch with a blanket, put the remote control for the television in my hand, and cooked me a meal. He did it selflessly to make me feel better. This was my boyfriend, the greatest guy I had ever met. To this day, he has never asked for anything in return, only my happiness and well-being.

Ronnie asked me to marry him on Christmas Eve, a little after two years of dating. When he got down on one knee and asked, "Will you marry me?" I couldn't say anything at first. All of those thoughts of me not being able to have a baby surfaced. Even though he and I talked about it at great length, and adopting was the plan once we were married, I still found myself wanting to remind him of the concern just to make sure he was still okay with it. I said, part nervous, part shocked. "But I can't have kids."

"I'm not marrying you for your reproductive system. I'm marrying you, Erin, for the whole person you are." He continued with a smile, "I'm on my knee waiting for an answer, will you marry me?"

I started crying, not sad, but happy, relieved tears and said, "Yes, of course I'll marry you!" Then we began to call our family and friends to tell them we were engaged.

It was a great night! After making phone calls to family and friends we knew we weren't going to see that night, we stopped off at the O'Briens' open-house Christmas gathering on the way to Aunt Nancy and Uncle Brian's annual Christmas Eve family party. I met the O'Brien family through Ronnie when Ronnie and I were just friends. As time went on they became more like family than friends. Ironically, one of Ronnie's best friends, Rob (who Ronnie told he was going to marry me the second time we met), married one of the O'Brien daughters, Moira.

When we walked into the party and announced that we just got engaged, Mr. and Mrs. O'Brien took out the video camera and the champagne and started videotaping the moment, while we all toasted to our engagement with a house full of guests. It was such a great feeling. The long, drawn out fear at age twenty-five of never having a serious relationship was such a waste of time. There I was, only a few years later, drinking champagne at the O'Briens' house, celebrating my engagement to be married.

After a while, we left their house (floating on air) and headed over to Aunt Nancy and Uncle Brian's, where the celebration continued. I have always loved Christmas Eve because my aunt and uncle throw a great party with awesome food and most of my family there to celebrate. Just when I think something can't get any better, it always seems to. Ronnie knew that Christmas Eve was a special night for me, so he picked the perfect night to propose. And to be able to share it with friends and family while still in shock made it all that much better.

During the engagement, there were so many details to take care of. As I said earlier, until I did it myself I did not fully grasp what it was like. The planning, registering, picking the right gown, trying to figure out who was sitting with whom, and so on seemed so surreal. It was so much fun! Sure there were stressful moments, and they caused me to lose a lot of weight, but I kept remembering those times when I had thought that these special occasions might never happen for me, which put everything right back into perspective. If I was having an extremely stressful time, Ronnie would remind me of the same. He and I wanted to enjoy the engagement and took our time picking out whatever we wanted for our special day. There I was, planning our wedding with my groom-to-be, cancer-free.

Ronnie and I married twenty months after the proposal, exactly four years from when we officially became "boyfriend and girlfriend" (on Saturday, August tenth) and three years after my treatments ended. We have an incredibly deep appreciation for the depth of our relationship based on its origin. We always talk about how we had the best time at our wedding. I married my best friend.

We went to Hawaii on our honeymoon and stopped off in California (Disney) for a few days to break up the flight on the way back. It was so relaxing and so much fun at the same time. After we came home and a couple of months went by, all of the weight that I had lost during the engagement came right back on. I was back to where I am supposed to be. For health reasons, I like to keep my weight at the average point that I spoke about earlier. This affords me twenty pounds to lose if, God forbid, I get sick. I believe that it's better to have and not need, then to need and not have.

After experiencing the debilitating, degrading, life-threatening circumstances of cancer, I developed an even stronger belief that the love of my life really was for better or worse, in sickness and in health. My appreciation for my husband goes so deep I can feel it in my soul. Thankfully, I went out on that limb and believed in myself. By doing so, I experienced the greatest free fall into love imaginable.

Perk 7
Having the Family They Thought I'd Never Have

God! Where do I begin? Throughout my ordeal, my faith in God was a source of comfort, and it gave me the confidence I needed to bear whatever came my way. My unconditional and complete faith in God provided the reassuring certainty that He will grant me the courage, strength, and will to get through anything. There is an old expression, "God will never give you more than He knows you can handle." Based on my experiences, nothing could be more true.

When I was first diagnosed, the doctors offered me the option of removing some of my eggs. They would freeze them for when I decided to have children. The doctors were concerned that I would not be able to conceive after the treatments, so this was their alternative. I was twenty-five years old, single, and my biggest concern prior to my diagnosis was what to wear on Friday night. I knew I did not want to get married before thirty, so the thought of children was the furthest thing from my mind. This being my state of mind and never having heard of such a procedure as "stored eggs,"

I found the whole idea disgusting. Not only was I repulsed by the thought of my eggs being stored somewhere, I would have had to pay rent for the safekeeping of my little goodies to boot. This, to me, was the craziest thing I had ever heard of.

There I was, in a large conference room in Memorial Sloan-Kettering Cancer Center, sitting at an extremely long table along with my parents, grandparents, Aunt Rita, and the team of doctors. I was sitting directly across from my ninety-year-old grandfather. He had such a sad, confused look on his face. I would reach across the table, hold his arm and say with a calming smile, "Don't worry, Grandpa, I'm going to be all right." When the doctors began their informative discussion, every time I saw my grandfather fidget, I'd remind him with a smile, "Remember, Grandpa, I'm telling you, I'm going to be fine."

Aside from the significance of the discourse, it was incredibly personal. We were discussing things I would never discuss in front of my father, grandfather, or any man for that matter. I come from a very conservative family. For example, God forbid someone said the word "period" when referring to the menstrual cycle—the whole family, especially my sister Katie, would run for cover. We referred to it as the "monthly thing." So you can only imagine my humiliation when having to discuss my period (sorry Katie-goo), menopause, freezing my eggs, my uterus, and anything else having to do with reproduction in front of my family and the doctors. Nevertheless, it had to be done. I refused their proposal with a look of disgust and a full-body shudder.

I had not given the idea of "stored eggs" any serious thought and continued on with my treatments. The emotional and psychological ramifications that decision had on my life just a few years later rocked my world.

When we were "just friends," Ronnie shared with me that he always dreamed of having a son. I wanted to try everything within my power to make his dream a reality. I prayed to God day and night asking Him to bless us with a child. Using visualization techniques, I projected the image in my mind's eye of us having a child. I refused to believe that I could not get pregnant, just like I refused to believe that I would not be cured of cancer. I prayed and prayed, in addition to the visualization technique, which I believe to be a gift from a higher power. It is almost as if the universe starts to direct you toward your visualized goal. I never gave up on the idea that, one day, we would have children.

My prayers continued, and the visualization became stronger and stronger. I knew in my heart and mind that we would have a child one day, regardless of what others thought. Although the odds were against us and the doctors disagreed, I had this unshakable feeling in my gut. My gut feelings have never been wrong. It was when I did not heed them that I ended up in trouble.

After Ronnie and I had been married for about five months, I moaned, "Pills, pills, pills. Ronnie, I am so sick of taking pills." According to the doctors, the birth-control pill would keep my cycle regular. It was one of the last few pills I had to take. I continued, "Let's see if my cycle is regular on its own. It'll be one less pill to worry about."

He agreed, and, thankfully, my cycle was just fine without that pill.

Approximately seven months after the wedding, we went to pick up our wedding album. The photographer was forty-five minutes from where we lived, so it was a bit of a ride. We picked up the pictures and dined at a nearby restaurant. We reminisced about how great both the wedding and the honeymoon were.

It was dark on the way home, but there were more stars in the sky than I had ever seen before. The moon was bright and seemed to follow us everywhere. It was a beautiful sight. I found myself, once again, staring at the sky and praying, *Please God, bless us with a child.* At that moment, I had a sinking feeling in my stomach. At first,

I figured it was indigestion, but this time it felt different. A few minutes later, I thought, *Could I be pregnant?* The thought was so overwhelming that I put it out of my head. The next morning I woke up and went to the gym for an early aerobics class. I did this class multiple times a week without a problem. Until now. I became lightheaded and had to go home. Once again I thought, *Could I be pregnant?* So, of course, I rushed to the pharmacy and bought a pregnancy test kit. And, guess what? It was positive! But I wouldn't allow myself to believe that we were going to have a baby until the blood test confirmed it. I called my gynecologist and she faxed over the script needed for the lab. The next day it was confirmed—*I was pregnant!*

I wanted to surprise Ronnie, so that night I went to the supermarket and bought foods pertaining to the word "baby." There were baby-back ribs, baby shrimp, and more. Once I told him, he was ecstatic. I don't recall a moment of our time together that I have ever seen him look so happy.

After dinner we started making phone calls to family and friends. Everyone was shocked. It was a miracle. When I called my mother and told her the good news, she asked, "Wha, wha, what did you just say?"

"I'm having a baby, Ma. I had the blood test and it's real."

"Oh, my God, Erin, I can't believe it. After everything you've been through...I'm so happy for you. I gotta go get your father. How far along are you?" she asked excitedly.

"I don't know; a couple of days or so?" I said, kidding around because I really didn't know at that point.

My mother and I continued to talk about the pregnancy and how ecstatic we both were. For me, the whole experience made my connection with my mother that much deeper. This is another example of how I never truly understood what others went through until I experienced it myself. I was still in shock. First the wedding, and now a baby the doctors thought I'd never have. It kept getting better and better!

After I told my parents (and my sisters were home as well), I called Aunt Rita. She screamed a happy scream that only Aunt Rita was capable of. It went something like this, "Aahh! Aahh! Aahh! (with deep breaths and some happy laughter between each scream) Erin you are an ox." She went on sounding so thrilled and amazed, talking about how after everything she saw me go through, I was able to have a baby. Aunt Rita was always my biggest cheerleader. She was always in my corner cheering me on. The news of me having a baby when it was against all odds had the two of us elated. We both knew I had managed to do something the doctors said would not happen, unless I stored my eggs.

When I hung up with Aunt Rita, the phone rang a few seconds later. It was my friend Barbara. I told her my good news and she was so excited for me. "You have to call my mother," she said. Just like I explained that the O'Briens are more like family than friends (I met them through Ronnie), the Jermyns are more like family than friends too (Ronnie met them through me). Mrs. Jermyn was thrilled for me. She had lymphoma after she had four children and she and I had the same internist and specialists. Mrs. Jermyn was not just my best friend's mother—because of our shared cancer experience, she was my friend as well. She and I stayed on the phone for quite a while talking about what a miracle it was and how wonderful that it was happening.

Everything was going along well until I was nine weeks pregnant. I had some bleeding. I called the ob/gyn at about three o'clock in the morning, crying uncontrollably. I said, "Doctor, I'm bleeding. I'm nine weeks pregnant with a baby that everyone including myself thought would never be. What do I do? Am I miscarrying? I can't deal with this! What do I do?"

The doctor told me to go for a sonogram in the morning, then see him in his office. This was not my main gynecologist whom I trust with my life, and my baby's as well. This was my introduction to the doctor on-call. He was great. He calmed me down and explained that my low-lying placenta was causing the bleeding. It was not a miscarriage. However, I had to be put on modified bed rest (I call it house arrest) until the medical problem resolved itself.

I'm not the type to just sit back and wait for things to resolve themselves, so I'm incredibly appreciative that my parents took very seriously the responsibility of instilling worthy ideals and values in me throughout my childhood. I was taught how important faith in God was and to embrace my faith wholeheartedly. I never could have imagined how fortunate I was that they impressed upon me the importance of faith until it was tested. It was nurtured deep within my soul, and I chose not to deny myself that gift. I feel faith became the most important force leading me along the path toward being cured of cancer, and getting me through this trying time with the pregnancy.

Just like when I had the cancer, there were so many nights when I lay awake, unable to organize my thoughts, much less put them into words. The fear, trepidation, and anxious stress I was experiencing were inexplicable. I could not express myself in words or thoughts. My communication process assumed a transcendental character. I knew that the only one in the position to comprehend the depth of my emotions was God. I knew He understood exactly how I felt both physically and emotionally. During those trying times, whatever feelings I could not express or explain, whether it be fear of dying from cancer or fear of losing my baby, I was relieved and reassured that my sensations were vented in some form. God became my confidant who helped me get through the turmoil.

I was not alone. My family and friends were there for me completely, but I had thoughts and emotions too complex to convey. If I was puzzled by my own experiences, how could I have expected others to understand?

Throughout all the confusion, though, something wonderful happened. Not only was I part of the church community, but God and I were working together one on one. We became best friends.

In addition to prayer, I used the visualization technique and envisioned the placenta moving up the uterine wall, holding on tight so it wouldn't dislodge causing a miscarriage. I used the same deep visualizing that I used with the cancer—strong, deep, meditative visualization of the placenta clinging to the wall of the uterus as it moved upward. Eventually, it did. When I went for my twenty-week sonogram, the low-lying placenta had moved to where it was supposed to be. But at the same time, the doctor informed me that I had too much amniotic fluid. It was back to house arrest for the duration of the pregnancy.

Ironically, after all of the concern of either a miscarriage or an early delivery, they had to induce me when I was five days late. Not only that, they had to manually deliver the placenta. This was something I had not encountered in *any* of the books I read preparing for delivery and beyond. *Yikes!* says it all. But for me, that experience reaffirmed how powerful the mind is.

I visualized so intensely, the same as I did when I had cancer, and the outcome was the same for both: positive and grateful. God blessed us with a gorgeous, healthy baby boy. The prayers, visualization technique, positive mind, and divine providence are what I believe gifted us with our son, Brendan Thomas Ley. Brendan Thomas was named after St. Brendan, the Irish explorer, and Thomas, after my cousin Tommy Joyce (a priest). My doctors refer to Brendan as the miracle baby. Four years later, my second miracle child, Daniel Joseph, was born. Ronnie and I both loved the name Danny, and Joseph is Ronnie and my father's middle name. Danny is also gorgeous and healthy, and proof that conceiving a child was no problem post-treatment, for me. Lastly, we welcomed our third miracle. Maggie Gabrielle came quickly thereafter, sixteen months after Danny to be exact, and she is named after my grandmother. Our children are very special, and I believe God has many great things in store for them.

In my opinion, life follows God's plan, and as part of my faith, I find that quite comforting.

In addition to prayer, there is hope. As a cancer patient, I hoped for one thing—a cure. I believed my cure would bring about good health and, in turn, reward me with the promise of life. With that life, I was able to go on and bring other lives into the world—my children. What a wonderful blessing which will never be taken for granted.

Without hope, my predicament would have been insoluble, hopeless. I do not think anyone struggling through a shipwreck-type situation chooses to be hopeless. I think it is born out of insecurity and lack of control. Feeling insecure and losing control were just side effects of my medical issues. They did not define who I was or my situation. Where there is life, there is hope! And I needed hope to reinforce my positive attitude and sense of humor. Hope is the equivalent of the light at the end of the tunnel. I kept my focus on that light, and it brought quality to my very existence. My shoulders dropped to where they belong, signifying relaxation, and before I knew it, I was smiling inside and out once again. I never gave up on hope or prayer, and I hope and pray that you won't either.

Conclusion
How Cancer Improved My Life

The expression "coming full circle" is so apropos in my situation, in that I have survived cancer, only to find myself in the beginning stages of someone else's diagnosis. For some unknown reason, I have been placed in the unique position of being able to provide the guidance sorely needed as these people try to work through their suffering.

Whether it is a family member, friend, neighbor, acquaintance, or even strangers across the nation, I have steered and will continue to steer those in need through the darkness of their new medical situation. To be able to lend a helping hand and lead them toward the proper medical attention, to provide some meaningful response to their questions and concerns, or even to have them struggle less as a result of our conversation, is a truly rewarding experience. I feel it is the least I can do.

When I came through, cancer-free, I felt privileged to have discovered the key to my life: never give up.

There were times during my protocol when I decided I needed to learn as much as I could about this dreaded disease that had my body under attack.

Any time there was a dilemma related to my situation, whether it related to oncology, gastroenterology, gynecology, pulmonology, endocrinology, neurology, or any other issue that arose as a result of my treatments, I asked as many questions as I thought to ask, to gain as much knowledge and understanding of my situation as possible.

Sometimes, while playing the role of detective, I found that the depth of knowledge and expertise among the many experts I encountered varied. In following the lead of the experts, I frequently found there was one who, more than the others, had insight or critical knowledge that made all the difference in the world at that time.

Now, I feel I know myself through and through. I knew I wanted my health, a loving family, husband, children, friends, peace of mind, and to always extend my hand and heart to those who need me. I am deserving of all of it, and it became my reality.

After having made this long journey, I can now detect, at the center of my being, a sense of wholeness and integration, where the physical, emotional, and spiritual all come together to yield a quiet calm and stillness. From it all I have attained a certain peace. I have regained my sense of self and all of the happiness that comes with it.

What started off as advice to my cousin Kathy when she was diagnosed with Hodgkins lymphoma has evolved into the consolidation of ideas and the development of this book. It has been referred to by some as a lifeline and I hope it will be just that for those of you who need it now, or will need it in the future.

Author's Note

Thank you for sharing this journey through cancer with me, with all its ups and downs. I feel blessed to have had this profound experience, and to be able to share it with you. My sincere hope is that this book will help individuals and their families find a way to cope with cancer and the many confused emotions that come with it.

Why wait for a crisis like cancer to love and respect yourself one hundred percent? That was one of the questions that I asked myself many times after I found my place of peace. My life is now full of dreams come true, and I hope that through this book I can help you survive and thrive after a cancer diagnosis. I would love to hear your story! Feel free to contact me anytime.

Please visit my website for a list of cancer-related websites for all ages, other information related to cancer and *The Will to Live: The Perks of Cancer through the Eyes of a Survivor*, and updates on when and where I will be speaking. I am available to make presentations in schools, colleges, and hospitals, as well as to other groups. I am also happy to participate in various events, book signings, and interviews. If you are interested, please contact me via my website.

Never give up hope, and never stop looking for that silver lining. I know your dreams can come true, too, if your mind, heart, and spirit are open to the possibilities.

All the best,
Erin
www.erinley.com